Standing Strong

Other books by Dr. Ray Guarendi
from EWTN Publishing:

*Raising Upright Kids in an Upside-Down World:
Defying the Anti-Parent Culture*

*Jesus, the Master Psychologist: Listen to Him*

*Thinking Like Jesus: The Psychology of a Faithful Disciple*

*Adoption: Should You, Could You, and Then What?
Straight Answers from a Psychologist and Adoptive Father of Ten*

*Living Calm: Mastering Anger and Frustration*

*Taught by Ten: A Psychologist Father Learns from His Ten Children*

*Simple Steps to a Stronger Marriage*

Dr. Ray Guarendi

# Standing Strong
## Good Discipline
## Makes Great Teens

EWTN Publishing, Inc.
Irondale, Alabama

EWTN Publishing, Inc.
5817 Old Leeds Road, Irondale, AL 35210

Distributed by Sophia Institute Press, Box 5284, Manchester, NH 03108.

paperback ISBN 978-1-68278-265-1

ebook ISBN 978-1-68278-266-8

Library of Congress Control Number: 2023946949

First printing

*To my wife, Randi, my soulmate and best friend,*
*who has taught me so much about family life*

# Contents

# Acknowledgments

Setting out to thank all who have, in any way, helped put together this book would create a list longer than the first chapter. You know who you are, so thank you all very much.

A few folks need to be mentioned by name. Thank you, Hannah, for all your typing of Dad's columns. You resisted the temptation to teach your siblings how to get around my discipline. Thank you, Sarah, for taking over from Hannah, as she quit typing for me just to go to college.

Thank you, Andrew, Jon, Joanna, Sammy, James, Mary, Peter, and Elizabeth, for volumes of good material. If this book sells well, your mother and I will get back some of the money that paid those exorbitant grocery bills you've brought upon us. And no whining that you got mentioned only in the acknowledgments. I dedicated the last book to all of you.

Thank you, Taylor Wilson and Devin Jones and my editors at EWTN and Sophia Institute Press, for being so professional and easy to work with.

Thank You, God, for the ability and the opportunity to do this again.

# Introduction

"When are you going to write a book about teenagers?" This is a question I've heard from parents for years with more than a touch of exasperation. As a father of ten children, six of them at one time teenagers, I can personally relate.

Indeed, the question reflects a certain level of struggle common to guiding and disciplining kids as they move through adolescence. Perhaps no other time of parenthood is so intense in its highs and lows, its frustrations and rewards, its sense of vulnerability and satisfaction.

Questions on discipline, setting limits, and supervision are far and away the ones I most receive from parents. The specifics change but not the essence: How can I be a stronger parent? What can I do to be more consistent? How closely do I supervise? Can I be too strict? How do I get more cooperation? More respect? A better attitude?

A common scenario occurs in my office. A parent will detail a litany of long-time unruly behavior from a teen but then add, "I think I'm giving you the wrong impression. Overall, he's a pretty good kid."

"How's that?"

"Well, he's not on drugs or anything like that. He doesn't give me the trouble some other parents are getting from their kids. I guess I should be grateful."

I ask, "What kind of adult do you want looking back at you at age twenty-two? How would you like to describe him? If you're satisfied to say, 'We've had our share of bad times, but he is finally starting to grow up,' you can parent like the crowd. Most parents don't raise seriously troubled kids who become seriously troubled adults.

"Or would you prefer to say, 'I'm not really objective, but he is a one-in-a-hundred kid. Morals, character, maturity, compassion—he is a beautiful human being'? Are you ready, then, to be a one-in-a-hundred parent? You will love, teach, and supervise well above most. You will discipline when other parents are lax. You will stand strong when many parents yield. You will teach standards that are exceptional. And, in the end, your children will most benefit."

This book is aimed at helping you raise someone who, at age twenty-two, will be seen by others, who are more objective than you, as a one-in-a-hundred young adult.

1

# The Beauty of the Beast

Every age has its own persona, and the teen years have a pretty negative one in the majority of folks' eyes. Put me in the minority. I think that teens get a bad rap. Sure, they can be argumentative, surly, and unappreciative at times — some might even say these are their better qualities. The real nature of the teen beast, though, is full of life, enthusiasm, energy, and laughter.

It's up to us parents to bring out our kids' natural best and not permit the worst to rule. Then we can honestly say to others' shock, "I really like these teen years."

# The Best Is Yet to Come

*Dear Dr. Ray,*

*I have three children, ages nine to twelve. If I hear one more time, "Enjoy them now. Soon they'll be teenagers," I think I'll scream. Are the teen years really all that unpleasant?*

*Bracing for What?*

If you polled a thousand parents, most would tag the teen years as the toughest, whether from personal or others' experience. If you took the same poll a hundred years ago, no doubt the numbers would look quite different. Isn't fourteen years old now the same as fourteen years old then? Have kids changed that much in just a few generations?

Yes and no. Physically, adolescence is a time of dramatic change. Hormones surge, bodies stretch, and kids want to be more grown-up than is good for them. So in that sense, yes, the typical teen pushes harder than the typical littler kid, sometimes with a relentless obnoxiousness new to the parent's experience. That acknowledged, my impression, stronger the longer I am a psychologist, is that modern-day teen turbulence is more cultural than developmental.

Once more, drop back a hundred years. How likely would the average farmer lament, "My boy turned fourteen last week. He's getting to be more of a teenager all the time. I can't get him to help around here as much as he used to, and he just wants to hang out with his buddies. All my friends have been getting the same kind of attitudes from their teenagers. I guess I just gotta ride it out."

---

## Modern-day teen turbulence is more cultural than developmental.

---

Not a likely scenario. First, *teenager* was not a word used in 1900. It's a recent description of a slice of childhood, complete with its own meaning and personality.

Second, that farmer was likely overjoyed about his son's getting older. The boy was becoming a young man, stronger and capable of a larger share in the family's welfare. "Older is harder" probably didn't cross the farmer's mind, or if it did, it was more than offset by "older is more helpful."

Was it the rural lifestyle causing dad to see his son as he did? Wouldn't the "city folks" see it more as we do today? Again, I don't think so.

In the past few generations, the lifestyle of the typical child has evolved into a fast-paced go-go, get-get, do-do, have-have. As kids move into adolescence, what they want to try, do, and possess spirals upward dramatically. Such is a recipe for family friction. The more stuff and perks a child sees as a given for growing up, the more "teenlike," if you will, he becomes if he doesn't get it. If a parent tries to slow the pace, especially more so than other parents are doing, discontent or surliness can follow.

Granted, this is only one factor of many different from raising kids a hundred years ago. But it's a potent one, more so than modern parents realize. Therefore, to better enjoy your kids as the teen years come and go, here are a few basics:

1. Give them less materially—sometimes far less—than you are able or than their peers get. Character is better shaped by less than by more.
2. Don't use their peers or their peers' parents as a guide to "normal" teen freedoms. The average teen with the average parents has too much freedom too early.
3. Always ask: Will this help or hurt my child's moral development? Err on the safe side.
4. Brace yourself for resistance and questioning. To teens "out of the norm" most often means "wrong," even when out of the norm is better than the norm.

So can you expect to enjoy the teen years, or will you have to endure them? Believe it or not, high standards will make not only for great adults someday but also for more pleasant kids along the way.

# He's the Nicest Boy

*Dear Dr. Ray,*

*My thirteen-year-old son is giving me a lot of discipline trouble. But everyone else – teachers, coaches, neighbors – says he is the nicest boy. What gives?*

*Is It Me?*

Don't worry. He probably just likes them better than you. Just teasing.

First of all, most kids are better behaved with others than with their parents. Indeed, aren't most people nicer with nonfamily than with family? It is a feature of relationships, albeit not a good one.

> Most kids are better behaved with others than with their parents.

Second, kids know their parents far better than they know anyone else. Consequently, your son knows, by living with you, what your habits are: what you'll allow, how you'll react, how long you'll persevere, when you'll finally wear down, what your mood is, how many times you'll nag or negotiate, when you've "had enough." Most likely, your son has formed a precise picture of who you are, and he acts accordingly.

Third, the majority of kids feel secure in their parents' love and acceptance. So they are more prone to act impulsively or obnoxiously or uncooperatively with them. They simply relax their inhibitions with those whom they love most and who love them most.

Fourth, most people make fewer demands of a child than does a parent. Therefore, others aren't as likely to receive much childish opposition. Good parents, however, have rules, chores, standards—you know, the stuff kids question. So good parents have to work harder at getting cooperation. Put another way, you provide many more opportunities for your son to push back on you.

Just because it's typical for kids to treat parents worse than others doesn't mean it's good or right. Parents routinely say, "Well, she gives me a lot of grief, but she's great with others. I must be doing something right." Yes and no. Yes, it's good that she treats others well. It shows she is absorbing good social sense. No, it's not a consolation for the mistreated parent.

Few give to a child what a loving parent does. You deserve all the respect and good treatment—and then some—that others are getting. Indeed, God declares parents so important that He's given them 10 percent of the commandments.

How a child treats a mother or father predicts how he will one day treat others. While he may respect others now, if he doesn't respect his family, he won't become morally mature enough to treat most anybody well.

Through his demeanor with others, your son is telling you something: He is quite capable of self-control and good conduct. If he can act so with others, he can act so with you. You may just have to alter how he perceives you.

For instance, if he knows you will debate and dispute, talk less and act more. If he reads you as inconsistent, get more predictable. If he sees your resolve as weak—well, you get the idea. In short, teach your son that you expect to be treated well, and back up your expectations with consequences.

In good homes, most often time closes the gap between how a child acts with his parents and how he acts with others. By the time he is seventy-four, he should be treating you okay. (Again, just kidding.) Nevertheless, a good parent doesn't wait passively for the gap to close. She makes it abundantly clear—with strong discipline, if necessary—that she will help a child "honor thy father and mother."

Then, when others says, "He's the nicest boy," you can honestly respond, "I think so too."

# After All I've Been for You

*Dear Dr. Ray,*

*My son, age sixteen, has the attitude "You say I'm a good kid, but it doesn't get me anywhere. I still don't have the freedom my friends have, and they give their parents a lot more trouble than I give you."*

*Ungrateful*

Pick one:
   A. After all I've done for you, Mother, this is the thanks
       I get.
   B. You should be grateful I'm not as bad as most kids.
   C. What do you want from me? I'm not on drugs, and I
       get good grades.
   D. I've had all kinds of chances to do bad things, and I
       haven't done them. What has it gotten me?
All are variants of a standard teen protest: "I'm playing by the rules, and you're still not easing the rules." Let's analyze each grievance.

"You say I'm a good kid, but it doesn't get me anywhere." Of course it does. It gets you good character and a safer, more stable adolescence. If being a good kid is only to get more freedom, more perks, and more goodies, then you're not yet being good for the right reasons. Besides, why give you more chances to make bad decisions and thus lose some of your good kidness?

"I still don't have the freedom my friends have." That is true. If I wanted my son to do and have what most kids do and have, I'd raise him that way. My decisions are based upon your welfare. I won't relax my standards simply because you've kept them. That's not good for you or me.

"They give their parents a lot more trouble than I give you." I can't know that for sure, but I'll take your word for it. And that just proves my point. You are who you are, in part, because we are who we are. Therefore, why would I want to change the very ways that helped me raise a son like you? I'm proud of you, and I want to stay proud. Your character is not measured by how you stack up against others. It's measured by how you act, independent of others.

> Why would I want to change the very ways
> that helped me raise a son like you?

Your son is echoing a modern moral high bar—that is, "I'm not on drugs." It claims, "Well, I could be a lot worse. At least I'm not as bad as that guy." As cultural morals decline, it's natural to believe that one, by comparison, sits morally upright.

Persevere in your above-the-norm standards, and your son should mature past his peer comparing and judge character by higher standards of right and wrong. After all, he is still a kid and, as he says, a pretty good one. He has time to become morally more clear-eyed.

Next time your son implies that you should be grateful, respond, "I am grateful. It could be a lot worse. After all, I'm not on drugs."

# Middle Child Syndrome

*Dear Dr. Ray,*

*I have three girls, ages ten, thirteen, and fifteen. Our middle daughter can be very difficult, much more so than her sisters. Lately I've read about "middle child syndrome," and some of its features sound like hers.*

*Middle Mom*

"Middle child syndrome" presents this picture: The middle child is lost in the family. He doesn't have the privileges given the oldest or the attention given the youngest. He's caught in between, unsure of how he fits into the family schemata. Consequently, he's prone to identity struggles and misbehavior, primarily to get attention, because he feels that bad attention is better than no attention.

There's only one thing wrong with the picture: It's false. Middle child syndrome doesn't exist. It's a faux disorder, largely concocted and profiled in the popular press. True, some middle kids do have identity or behavior problems, but so do some oldest kids, some youngest kids, some only kids, and some second-from-the-last fraternal twins.

> Middle child syndrome is a faux disorder, largely concocted and profiled in the popular press.

Tongue planted firmly in cheek, I advise parents, "If you fear middle child syndrome, don't have an odd number of kids. If you already have three or five, have another. Eliminate that middle spot." If you have seven, nine, or eleven, middle child syndrome is probably the least of your worries.

In fact, the research on birth-order effects is inconsistent and inconclusive. Rather than a child's place in the family order bringing with it certain characteristics, birth order has a negligible effect, if any, on a child. The only research with some consistency centers on oldest or only children. As a group, they tend to be slightly more independent and achieving. And is that due to their position or our evolving style?

With our first child, we boil everything that comes within fifty feet of her. By the time the last child rolls around, we throw her a big dirtball and say, "Here, chew on this. And wipe your mouth off on the grass before you come into the house."

The first child has triple pictures of every burp and potty visit. The last child has one picture from the hospital and one from his wedding rehearsal dinner. And when he finally notices, "How come I have no pictures, Mom?" we fudge, "That's not true. Your sister did a popsicle sketch of you in first grade. We kept it. Besides, you look like your sister. Use her pictures."

It sounds as if your daughter is struggling harder than her sisters to grow up, and possibly some of this is related to her middle spot. But likely it is due to something more influential: her temperament—her wiring, if you will. That she's your middle daughter may be coincidental. She very well could act the same, no matter her family position, because of her inborn personality.

You may still have to deal with your daughter's "extra" troubles on her way to adulthood. But she doesn't have a "syndrome." She's uniquely she, and you, being her mother (are you an only mom or a middle mom?), are in the first position of helping her mature.

How long must a child live in the middle to contract MCS (you know a disorder has arrived when you can call it by its initials)? My daughter was our middle child for two years until we adopted our son (child number four). Is MCS something she'll outgrow, or will she always be a middle child at heart?

As my wife and I moved our way up to being parents of many, we had four different middle children. Which raises the question: How long does a child have to be in a middle to develop "middle child syndrome"?

# The Letter Phenomenon

*Dear Dr. Ray,*

*What do you think about all the diagnoses that children are labeled with? It seems new "disorders" are popping up almost every day.*

*Letter Alone*

Pick a child, any child. Don't raise him well. Lack love. Drag him through adult-created chaos and turbulence. Expose him early and often to toxic media and entertainment.

Or love him lots but discipline him little. Be permissive, erratic, or weak. Overindulge, give too much of everything — freedom, perks, goodies. For whatever the reason, from malignant neglect to spoiled-rotten indulgence, don't consistently, resolutely teach morals and character.

As the child grows, his socialization doesn't keep pace. Consequently, he can display much that is ugly: immature, nasty, violent, bizarre, inexplicable, or conscienceless conduct.

Then come the questions: What is wrong here? Why is this child acting this way? Is there a psychological problem? An emotional disorder? Unresolved anger? Deep-seated disturbance?

Professional analysis often follows and, in so many words, concludes, "Yes, after evaluating this child, I've determined he does appear disordered. He has letters. He has ODD, ADD, ADHD, LSMFT, IRS, EIEIO." The letters gather, all attempting to explain what's wrong with this youngster.

Don't misread me: Legitimate diagnoses do exist. In my experience, however, these diagnoses are being grossly overused. They are pinned on too many kids, too easily, too quickly. Much lies in how they are defined, as boundaries are often vague and subjective. We adopted our son Jon when he was four. His womb life and early months were marked by drug exposure and neglect. As a toddler, he was placed in foster care, where he was well cared for but disciplined poorly.

During our early visits with Jon, among ongoing misconduct, he punched me in the face, attempted to strangle my wife, and kicked the foster father at random. His behavior was unlikable and unruly. As expected, the letters started in an attempt to understand Jon psychologically.

Many years later, none of those early letters remain except those I gave Jon when I first met him: Behaviorally Regressive Attitudinal Trauma (BRAT). Yes, Jon looked as if he was disturbed, but the cause was that he had not been disciplined or socialized well. Today Jon is showing who he really is: a young man with a sociable way—a way that had been buried for some time beneath an early ball of ugly behavior and habits. That was his problem, not a mental disorder.

> I diagnosed Behaviorally Regressive
> Attitudinal Trauma (BRAT).

If grown-ups don't do what is needed to love, teach, and discipline a child, the child can reflect the absence—although many children actually mature far better than they've been raised. Little Conan exhibits problems, to be sure, but they are not innate to him.

In other words, the parents didn't get cursed with a demon seed that nobody short of God could raise. Far more often, the child is only doing what he's learned, given a lack of nurturing or control.

So the proliferation of diagnoses placed upon children is, in large part, I believe, a consequence of family fragmentation, moral chaos, and indulgent permissiveness in various combinations. True, not all diagnoses are questionable, but a significant number are better explained as big people–little people dynamics rather than as some internal disruption afflicting the child.

# Attention-Starved?

*Dear Dr. Ray,*

*What do you think of the idea that kids misbehave to get attention; therefore, if a parent ignores bad behavior, it will go away?*

*Ignore-ant*

That notion is one I was nursed on educationally. Fortunately, I didn't pay much attention to it then, even less so now.

Here's its gist:

1. Kids want attention.
2. They'll find ways to get it.
3. Bad attention is better than no attention.
4. Acting bad will force grown-ups to pay attention.
5. Discipline is the price to pay for attention.

Plausible-sounding but, for the most part, faulty. Kids do want attention, and they will push for as much as they can get. It does not follow, however, that the main motive for Tallulah's misbehavior is to force attention. Most kids, as studies suggest, misbehave for one psychologically complex reason: They want to do what they want to do. Indeed, don't we all?

Motives for misbehavior are nearly endless: impulse, frustration, control, deception, manipulation, aggression. (Sounds like the promo for an upcoming miniseries.) Most children quickly realize that grabbing attention is not a priority motive for acting up, especially if it comes as discipline.

True, kids *can* misbehave for attention or what they can gain from the resultant upheaval or control or parental agitation. But these are effects, not necessarily causes.

In loving homes, deficient attention is not usually a driver of misbehavior; in fact, it's often just the opposite. Attention is what's keeping the trouble rolling.

Suppose Holmes is arguing for permission to go to Watson's house. Neither his homework nor his chores (do kids still have such prehistoric things as chores?) have been started, much less completed. The more you debate over why he can't leave, the longer he'll engage and the hotter the exchange. After twenty-seven minutes of word wrestling, will you end with, "Holmes, we've been interfacing for nearly half an hour, and I must admit, I'm beginning to experience some anger"?

Your point-counterpoint is ongoing attention. The argument will subside only when you refuse further negotiation or tell Holmes that any more debate will lead to an automatic no, extra chores, or an early bedtime.

"Misbehavior for attention" is effective in heaping guilt on good parents. If Tallulah is acting up just to get attention, does this mean she's not getting enough from you? Is your parenthood lacking? Is her obnoxiousness all your fault? Maybe you're just too oblivious or self-absorbed to raise an attention-satisfied kid.

Nonsense. Good parents give plenty of attention—maybe not all a child wants, but what children want is not always good for them. Some kids are attention seekers because they get too much to begin with.

If attention is not the motive for misbehavior, ignoring it won't stop it. Most misconduct has to be actively dealt with to reduce it.

A law of discipline: the more passive, the longer it takes to work. You may not yield to the demands of a temper fit as you attempt, however vainly, to tune it out, but you are also doing little about Stormy's rudeness or nastiness. Discipline works more quickly when a parent doesn't ignore but acts decisively and firmly.

One last logic problem: If Harmony is truly acting up to gain your attention and you don't give it, why then wouldn't she escalate her misconduct until she gets it? If 90-decibel screaming evokes no reaction from you, why not kick it up to 110 and see what happens?

If x amount of misconduct doesn't force you to respond, why not go to 2x or add y?

Sometimes it seems that kids are too smart for our theories. I just don't pay much attention to those theories.

# Forced Contact

*Dear Dr. Ray,*

*My thirteen- and fourteen-year-olds, who used to enjoy being with my husband and me, are becoming more reluctant to go anywhere with us. They always seem to have "something better" to do. Should we force the issue?*

*A Twosome Again*

Ah, sweet parental revenge. During the first nine or ten years of life, the kids embarrass us in public; after that, we embarrass them.

"Ah, c'mon, Dad, don't wear the shorts with the feathers again."

"Mom, please don't smile at me when other people are looking."

"Just drop me off here; I'll walk the last couple miles."

Listening to grandparents, I've come to believe that the great adolescent aversion to being with us dorky grown-ups is more social than developmental, if not more so. In the not-so-long-ago, double-digit age did not bring resistance to public parental contact. Only as life has become more frenetic and entertaining for kids has the competition for family time exploded.

Why should Freeman want to go out to eat with his mom — a high-level treat a few generations back — when he can call friends, surf the TV's 592 channels, play 37 computer games, or get picked up by Harley, who has a bigger TV, 3-D video games, and a cute sister who also sheltered at home to dodge her parents? It's not always that your kids aren't pulled to be with you; it's that the pull to be elsewhere is stronger. As their entertainment options exponentially expand with age, former top-ten pick—being with Mom and Pop—drops to number forty-seven.

Experts solemnly intone: It is normal and healthy for adolescents to separate from adults and to assert their autonomy in the development of independence—or some such psycho-verbiage. I'll bet their kids don't want to be with them either. Certainly, some separation is to be expected. But how has wanting to spend little time with one's parents come to be labeled healthy, developmentally speaking?

Further, just because something is to be expected doesn't mean it's to be welcomed or is good. It also doesn't mean you have to let it dictate family life.

What do you gain by forcing Freeman to attend his sister Noel's Christmas play or to visit elderly Aunt Agatha, who always cries when she sees how big he's getting and who wants to hug and kiss him goodbye and give him a dollar? I mean, how much trauma can he take?

The answer depends on what you want to teach Freeman. If you don't mind that he chooses teen freedom over family, then let him choose his pursuits. In the meantime, don't listen to the song "Cat's in the Cradle"; it could make you nervous.

On the other hand, if you want to teach Freeman that some things are more important than entertaining himself, then at times you will need to insist he go your way instead of his. Is it hard to figure in which way I go?

You might counter, "We do spend home time together." At that, if you're like most families, even home time is at a premium. Why give a teen the authority to reduce further what little family time you have? More importantly, not all lessons in character are taught at home. A visit to Aunt Agatha's, however boring in teen eyes, can teach manners, sacrifice, respect for elders, and compassion.

So do you hog-tie your kids and drag them kicking and screaming with you everywhere? Would you even want to do that? I don't
think so. It's wise, however, to judge together time on its merits
and not on whether your kids want it.

Sometimes good times emerge because parents insist on togetherness. Once past their resistance, the kids find that this time isn't
all so bad, assuming, of course, you change your shorts and don't
do anything too uncool, like snort when you laugh. And even if
your children don't willingly cooperate now, chances are they'll
see it differently someday. Many young adults now look back with
gratitude for those times of forced family contact, as they made
for forever memories.

# Hyper-Activitied

*Dear Dr. Ray,*

*What do you think of the activity flurry of families today, running endlessly from meeting to game to event?*

*The Taxi*

Your question has been sitting on my desk for months. I finally got to it while sitting in the car, picking up my son from ball practice early because my daughter's skating lessons were canceled. Or was it during my youngest son's soccer-game rain delay?

It's obvious, families have become more hyperactive in just the last few decades. The phenomenon is captured in those Christmas newsletters sent around at year's end. I suspect the updates are needed because no one saw each other much in the past twelve months. Too busy.

"Our daughter Mackenzie, now eleven, just finished her twelfth consecutive year of ballet, gymnastics, competition powerlifting, and ancient Semitic language scholarship. After her 2008 Olympic tryouts, she will be seeking a junior ambassadorship to NATO. And little Marshall, who just turned six, earned his black belt in karate, added sax as his third instrument of choice, and took first place in the National Spelling Bee. I'm trying to stay busy with ..."

The activities acceleration is the pursuit of the good at the cost of the best. Certainly sports, music, clubs, and interests all provide positives for kids. The trap for most parents lies in learning the balance between flurry and family, between pace and peace. Little

League ball for six-year-olds can be fun but not when it requires two games a week with practices on all off days.

The activities acceleration
is the pursuit of the good
at the cost of the best.

One mother told me that, upon realizing that she had been pulled into a speeding treadmill, she said to her two adolescent sons, "During your baths tonight, decide which two activities you wish to keep. The rest will be discontinued." She was regaining control over the flow of her family. A few weeks later, the boys were no worse for lack of wear; they were also more settled.

Families need open time, lots of it. It is in open time when good times spontaneously happen: a giggling conversation, an impromptu ice cream trip, sitting and teasing in the kitchen, a cutthroat game of "Trivia." Negotiable time is the stuff of closeness.

How do you know you're pursuing the good but losing some of the best?

1. Do you have a nagging sense that your family time is being gobbled up, either in the schedule of events or their juggling?
2. How often do you eat together as a family? Does someone always have someplace to be?
3. Do your kids routinely complain about being bored? Ironically, the more we jam each minute, the faster we become bored.
4. When was the last time two days went by without a scheduled activity?

5. Can you and your spouse regularly attend the kids' events together, or do you have to split your audience?

By the way, I was just kidding about writing this while sitting in the car. I wrote it at home, while my wife was sitting at soccer practice, just before she had to drop Sarah off at her violin lesson.

## 2

# We Just Don't Talk Anymore

No end of books have been written on the art of communicating with teens, if only the kids would read them. Most, if not all, repeat the same theme: Grown-ups need to talk and listen better so the kids will hear and understand better.

The message is not subtle: If your kids aren't hearing you, obviously your communication skills are lacking. If you were more skilled, every so often you'd be rewarded with "Oh, Mother, thank you. I've been so stubborn. Now I see what you're saying. That's why you're the parent and I'm the child. Can we hold hands and sing 'Kumbaya' around the campfire?"

In any interaction with teens, there's an unpredictable variable: the teens—which means that sometimes the best approach is knowing when to quit communicating.

Communication is most effective when all parties are reasonable. Need I say more?

# Somebody Speak to Me

*Dear Dr. Ray,*

*My kids and I could always talk. They're teenagers now, and I can't seem to get through to them on much of anything. Any ideas?*

*Talk to Me*

Your question, no doubt, has baffled countless parents over countless generations. I can imagine fathers everywhere thousands of years ago lamenting, "These kids nowadays. All they want to do is wear shoes. I tell them, these things are a passing fad. But do they listen?"

Most kids eventually do listen and, for the most part, emerge more open-minded. To paraphrase Mark Twain, "When I was fifteen, my father was the dumbest man in the world. Amazing how much smarter he got by the time I was twenty-one."

To enhance your credibility, here are some basic don'ts and do's for better reaching teens:

*Don't lecture.* Teens have a very strict definition of *lecture.* A lecture is: (1) any sentence over seven words, (2) any compound sentence, (3) any bunch of words beginning with "When I was your age," "Now listen here," "And another thing," "Let me tell you something," or, "You know, I wasn't born yesterday."

Teens reflexively shut down soon into a lecture. Eyes glaze, faces go slack, and they cease to register any incoming information except, "Do you have anything to say?" To which they reply, "Nuh uh."

Parents define *lecture* much more flexibly. We allow ourselves upwards of fifty thousand words before thinking we're lecturing. If we want to be better heard, we'd best gauge when to end the word count.

*Don't compare childhoods.* Our kids believe that our childhood has no relevance to them whatsoever. Whatever our point, it's lost on them because they know that all we really had to worry about was not being a dinosaur meal as we walked on all fours through six miles of overgrown jungle full of snakes and spiders. And we were grateful children.

Talking the present works better: "I'm not letting you go to Snake's party because I don't think there will be enough supervision." You may not be any more understood, but at least you won't get a look that says, "Tape Number 102: I didn't date your mother until we were engaged …"

*Don't try to resolve everything in the heat of the moment.* That, though, is the very moment we feel most pressured to make it absolutely clear what we think about finding a pack of cigarettes in Winston's coat pocket. His defense: "I'm holding them for my girlfriend, Salem." We know otherwise, but for the meanwhile, it might be a drag to keep repeating our arguments.

For one thing, Winston knows our stance on smoking; he's lived with us for fifteen years. For another, when all parties are calmer, clearing the air is more likely. Explosions don't clear the air; they cloud it.

*Do ask questions.* Understandably we have an overpowering urge to straighten out Oxford's wayward thinking when he reassures us that getting Cs and Ds as a freshman is smart: Then he can improve his grades late in high school and people will think he's getting smarter. Asking a few questions—What will colleges think? What do you think I'll do about your Cs and Ds?—may prompt Oxford to see the shortsightedness in his reasoning. That's a maybe.

*Do let some subjects ride.* Sixteen-year-old Maynard shares a revelation: "Mom, Roscoe's brother has a friend whose cousin's neighbor sold Christmas cards last month, and he made two thousand dollars. I could do that and just skip college."

Your first impulse: "Oh, so you think Christmas rolls around every month, and you can build a future selling cards?" Hold off for a day—okay, an hour. So long as Maynard keeps his grades up, just in case he changes heart and leans toward college, it's not urgent to challenge his career choice yet. He could sidle in three days from now with "Mom, I changed my mind. I want to be a brain surgeon." Then your impulse will be "You think you can get into medical school with those grades?" With teens, sometimes the best way to be heard is not to talk for a while.

*Do plant a seed.* Faith's friend isn't a friend in your opinion. She takes advantage of your daughter's trusting nature, but Faith hasn't noticed that yet. One day, Faith tells you how surprised she is that Jewel has no intention of repaying her the ten dollars she borrowed. Instead of "I was wondering when you'd find out what she was really like," try "Friends need to be picked carefully," or, "Sometimes people don't act the way we thought they would."

You've planted a seed for thought, and Faith will more likely mull that over than any "I told you so." A seed needs time to take root. If Jewel is a fake friend, Faith will bring up the matter again.

*Do be ready to listen.* When the emotion hits, even adolescents want to talk, even to us parents, even if because we're the only ones around. Most things that occupy us can be set aside for the meantime.

---

When the emotion hits, even adolescents want to talk, even to us parents, even if because we're the only ones around.

---

Communicating with adolescents can sometimes be as fruitful as running headlong into a brick wall. I don't know about you, but I had bricks in my makeup once. I still have some.

There is further benefit to listening: What we hear may scare us enough to appreciate a little ignorance.

# Listening Stamina

*Dear Dr. Ray,*

*My thirteen-year-old daughter complains that I don't listen long enough before giving my opinions. How can I listen longer?*

*Listening*

A remarkable coincidence (or maybe some farsighted linguist planned it so) is that *listen* and *silent* contain the same letters. Good listening begins with silence. The fewer words we interject while someone is voicing her thoughts, the more thoughts we'll hear.

Alas, holding our tongue is much easier to talk about than to do, especially as it's worrisomely clear that what we're about to hear we're not about to like. Sometimes the kids are talking on impulse: "Mom, I think I'm going to move to the South Pole when I'm eighteen. The solitude will help me find myself." Sometimes they're sounding foreboding: "Dad, you may be getting a letter from school tomorrow." Sometimes their words are pure fancy: "You know, schools should offer swing shifts, like factories. I'd get better grades on midnights."

Whatever the message, after hearing about six words, most of us are ready to unleash a torrent of commentary. We're driven by the fear that if Watson's elementary reasoning continues unchallenged for more than a few minutes, it will lock in.

To prolong your listening stamina, start with this: Nothing is made worse by listening. Even if Perry already has mapped out his itinerary to the South Pole, he hasn't left yet. There's still time to explore the details of his excursion. Who knows? As he talks on, he may raise the same questions you would. Similarly, if Stanford already has skipped the classes that generated the letter from school, he can't be skipping any more while he's standing in front of you, not unless he's incredibly ingenious.

To prolong your listening stamina,
start with this:
Nothing is made worse by listening.

As long as your daughter is talking and you're listening, nothing bad is happening. One parent said she felt fully secure only when her son was talking to her. Whatever he was saying, he wasn't out somewhere doing it.

A personal gag order is another way to listen longer. No comments or opinions for, say, one minute. If one minute of silence for you would be comparable to running a marathon race the first morning you take up jogging, start easy. Begin with twenty seconds or roughly the amount of time your daughter takes to walk into a room, look at you, and say, "Mom, if I tell you something, promise you won't get mad?"

Quiet attentiveness can compel kids to talk. Our silence creates a word void that can be unsettling, and they may feel the urge to fill that void. In other words, they may crack before we do.

Good listening begins with silence and moves to understanding. One father would say little until his son finished talking, whereupon Dad would paraphrase what he heard to make sure he heard it correctly. A mother preferred the "five W" approach with her ten-year-old: who, what, when, where, why. Only when she knew all five answers would Mom give an opinion, advice, or discipline.

There's an old saying: It is better to keep your mouth shut and let someone think you're dumb than to open it and remove all doubt. The person who said this must have had children. The longer we listen, the more we'll speak with credibility and authority when we do speak.

# The Quality Is in the Quantity

*Dear Dr. Ray,*

*What is your opinion of "quality time"?*

*Clock-watcher*

"Quality time" was conceived in the minds of experts who asserted, "It doesn't matter how much time you spend with children as long as it's good time." Just make sure that your moments with Daley are as mutually fulfilling as possible, and you needn't be too concerned about how many. Or, it's the quality, not the quantity, that counts.

Of course, positive time with kids is better than negative time. If 61 percent of your minutes with Melody are spent in disharmony, you might be wise temporarily to lessen your contact. Periodic separation may serve to salve the relationship.

If quality time is defined as time spent enjoying each other's company, few would dispute that this is good. The imbalance lies in quality replacing quantity.

First, quality is a slippery concept. It doesn't plug easily into a timetable. The older a child, the harder to get cooperation with our schedule of quality programming. Today's teens have so much mobility that they might only have an opening next Sunday night at 11:45. Quantity time allows the parent to do the booking.

Second, *quality time* all too often means entertainment time. We plan some activity with our youngster so we can "share the experience." But quality comes in many forms. When a grown daughter was asked what she remembered most about her father, she said it wasn't so much events or activities with him that stood out. Rather, he was just always there for her.

While *quality time* conjures up "interaction," warm moments can come from a parent's passive presence. One father said, "If the kids are playing in the family room, I'll move to the family room and read there, instead of reading in the kitchen." He didn't play or talk with them even; he just moved closer. It was his way of saying, "I'm right here, kids."

Quantity time prompts spontaneity—a post-bedtime snack, a tickle tangle on the couch, a late-night after-date talk. Quality needs quantity as a partner. The relationship is simple: the more quantity, the more quality.

One parent, looking back over two decades of motherhood, said, "Parents and kids need more time to be bored together." What? Seeking boredom when the culture says, "Act, move, do—now"? Boredom has value in and of itself. It slows the pace. It creates memories woven in love.

If quantity time matters so much, why has the concept of quality time risen so fast? Quality time is a by-product of a society on the run and wanting to justify itself with its children. Kids are blessedly flexible and resilient, and in the short term, they will allow us to skimp on them. In the long-term, we and they risk losing those sometimes we can't get back. If our lives are stuffed full, there is much to cut out that is far less essential than our children.

Reality always wins. And reality says that time is indispensable to high-quality parenting. Time is the framework upon which so much of family is built. It takes time to discipline well. It takes time to catch teens in the mood to talk with us. It takes time to teach, hug, pray, cry, be mutually frustrated, and then make up.

No matter how high the quality, it alone cannot form the bonds of a relationship. That takes quantity. It always will.

# Parents Are from Venus

*Dear Dr. Ray,*

*I try hard to understand my teenager's feelings, but whenever I stand my discipline ground, I hear, "You never listen" or "You just don't understand." What am I doing wrong?*

*I Do Understand*

Probably nothing. For a couple of generations now, the experts have hammered parents about the dangers of being communication Neanderthals and about the "how to" magic of being psychologically savvy listeners. Thus, many wonder, "What's wrong?" when their kids accuse them of being hard-hearted, hardheaded autocrats who would flunk a communication 101 course.

A hundred years ago, on the spot where I live sat a farm. That farm mom had a 5 percent chance of having a high school diploma. But she could have instinctively told you, "Kids don't understand or like much of what you do as a parent. They will someday, and that's what counts."

Nowadays parents are made to feel incompetent—communication challenged—if Sherlock doesn't understand them. Obviously, they're listening passively instead of listening actively. They're using a "you message" when an "I message" is called for. Their positive-to-negative statement ratio is only three-to-one instead of the ideal seven-to-one.

Certainly, parents can communicate poorly; teens can bring out our listening worst. And certainly, there are plenty of ways to make an exchange go sour. But when a parent is trying valiantly to understand the child, more often than not, it is the child who is being unreasonable rather than the parent.

When Holmes accuses, "You never listen to me," or Harmony whines, "Just once I wish you would see my side," quite often a parent has listened empathetically, with heroic patience even. In the end she just didn't change her mind, thus provoking recriminations.

The only foolproof way to always be perceived as a perfect listener is to give your teen exactly what she wants. "You mean you'd like to go to the mall unsupervised with your friends Rob and Chase? Of course." "I hear you, Stanford. You want to do your homework after 9:30 p.m., when you're more rested? Why didn't you just say so?" "Let me see if I understand, Ford. You're asking to borrow my car to take five friends to the state cage wrestling matches? Well, sure. Let it never be said that I'm not an open-minded parent."

> The only foolproof way to be perceived as an awesome listener is to give your teen exactly what she wants.

Unfortunately, the cost of avoiding the poor-listener tag—that is, giving in—is way too high for both parent and child. Better to listen however long you see fit and then quietly end with "I understand your point, but I don't agree with it. And I have to do what's best for you because I love you." That "love line" really makes kids mad, because down deep they know you mean it.

Active listening, to use modern psychospeak, means hearing what another is really saying. Okay, then, what Oral is really saying with "You don't listen"? Could it be "Why aren't you changing your mind?" So next time you get charged with "You never listen," do some active listening. "What I'm hearing you say is I'm not hearing what you're saying." So you see, even when you're "not listening," you're actually therapeutically listening.

Tricky stuff, this psychology.

# With Respect to Feelings

*Dear Dr. Ray,*

*I encourage my children (ages ten, twelve, and fifteen) to express themselves, but sometimes they get pretty nasty. I want communication, but I don't want disrespect. Is there one without the other?*

*Listening Too Much?*

If there isn't, tact and diplomacy are headed the way of chivalry.

Encouraging some freedom of expression promotes two-way respect. A youngster feels he receives a fair hearing, and a parent feels fairer for it. Allowing unrestrained freedom of expression promotes two-way disrespect. Burne may heat up the exchange, but soon we're matching hot word for hot word. Even if we start calm, we can't withstand open assault for long. Our desire for self-respect will overcome our desire for open communication. Communication without rules doesn't foster connection; it hurts it.

Good communication does not mean license to speak one's mind in whatever words at whatever volume with whatever tone. Freedom of opinion is benevolent parenthood; freedom of expression is not.

As children move deeper into adolescence, they become more deeply opinionated, particularly about what makes for acceptable parenting. Therefore, to establish some freedom of speech, in order to promote the general welfare and to semi-ensure domestic tranquility, some guidelines are in order.

1. Anyone can say his or her piece as long as it's said peacefully.
2. The speaker has the right to remain uninterrupted as long as he or she remains respectful.
3. As soon as expression turns ugly, the right to be heard is temporarily forfeited.

A major clarification: What constitutes disrespect is your judgment. Kids have a much more tolerant definition of disrespect than we do. They don't consider themselves disrespectful until they're tipping tables and tossing bricks—and then only if they hit something.

The simplest way to deal with ugly talk is to call a halt to it. In Congress, this is called invoking cloture. (I think it comes from the Old English phrase "Cloture mouth.") For a list of expression-halting consequences, refer to chapter 4, on reducing back talk.

---

Just because a rule is fair and
makes for more freedom,
that doesn't mean that kids will like it.

---

After all your explanations, after your heroic refusal to respond in kind—or in unkind—to disrespect, don't be too surprised if your children still believe you're stifling their First Amendment rights. Just because a rule is fair and makes for more freedom, that doesn't mean that kids will like it. It takes maturity to understand the benefit of such things as restraint and tact.

Here's a bright side: The kids can take advantage of your new guidelines to tell you what they think of your new guidelines—if they do it respectfully.

# Word Storms

*Dear Dr. Ray,*

*I'm a lecturer, and the kids are tuning me out. Is there hope to be heard?*

*Out of Tune*

In the book *Back to the Family*, David Paul Eich and I interviewed parents of strong families to find out what they were doing right. We also asked the kids what they liked and didn't like about their family life. For the teens, lectures ranked near the top of the "don't like" list. Routinely they admitted to drifting into a semiconscious state about two minutes into a steady word stream.

The propensity to lecture is understandable, beginning early in parenthood. When my oldest son was about four, my wife sent him to his bed for lying. Hearing from her what had happened, I decided to go into his room and add my fatherly two cents' worth, although I think the average lecture is about sixty-eight cents' worth.

"Andrew, Mom says you lied."

"I don't remember."

"Andrew, if Mom says you lied, you lied. Now, I'm going to ask you only once. If you tell me the truth, you'll stay here as long as Mom said. If you lie to me too, you'll stay here even longer. Now, did you lie?"

The silence was broken by the sound of mental wheels spinning.

"I still don't remember, but if Mom says I did, there's probably a pretty good chance I did."

The parenting passage I'd been anticipating: my first chance to lecture, though I'm sure that's not what I would have called it.

"Andrew, I want to talk with you a minute." Whereupon I gave him my best stuff—talking about trust, about God's rules about lying, about love. I shared a touching story from my own childhood. Our souls had met. Andrew would carry this moment with Dad for life.

About eight minutes into my monologue and his silence, I stopped. "Well, Andrew, what do you think?"

"Dad?"

"Yes?"

"How come if I look up at the ceiling with one eye, my other eye can't look at the floor?"

Somewhere in my soul talk, I lost that boy, and I think it was probably when I said, "Andrew, I want to talk with you a minute."

Why do we talk on in the face of gathering evidence that we're being tuned out, especially with teens, who can turn to stone at will? It relates to our diligent drive to be good parents. We desperately want to make ourselves understood. We know why Rock shouldn't punch Bruno tomorrow at school. If we can just get him to listen, he'll rethink, adding a "Golly, Dad, thank you for talking at me for thirty-seven straight minutes. I needed that."

---

If we can just get through to him, he'll rethink, adding a "Golly, Dad, thank you for talking at me for thirty-seven straight minutes. I needed that."

---

Why do lectures drift toward the futile?

One, kids don't see parenthood through our eyes. Densely packed parenting words, however persuasive to us, don't do much to convince kids to think as adults. Someday most will, when they're the ones lecturing.

Two, nobody—child or adult—likes to be on the receiving end of a droning. Further, while a lecture may start slow and low, it doesn't always stay that way. The longer it goes, the more likely it will move to a tirade.

Three, lectures are generally spawned by troublesome circumstances. Somebody—usually a juvenile—has behaved poorly, and somebody else—usually a parent—is really upset, hurt, or disappointed about it. The closer in time the lecture is to the trouble, the more likely emotions are to rule the moment.

Once in a while, lectures may be heard and heeded, but as a rule, the more words, the less impact. Options:

First, if you do lecture, keep it short. A short lecture couldn't be called a lecture. Two to three minutes should be enough to make your position clear.

Second, finish by explaining what you plan to do. Talking consequences keeps a lecture from getting personal.

Lastly, if your emotions are churning, delay the talk. Send Echo someplace else while you cool. With lower emotional temperatures come less-steamy words.

Thank you for listening. I was hoping you would, though sometimes I'm disappointed in how you react. After all I write for you, you'd think you'd care enough to read it. You know, not everybody is going to write for you all your life. You'd better get used to that fact because I'm going to tell you something else. When I was your age . . .

# Teen Tension

*Dear Dr. Ray,*

*Please give me some ideas for getting out of arguments with my teenagers.*
*I never win anyway.*

*Outwitted*

By definition, an argument involves two or more parties with
conflicting views. So to end arguments with teens, you can:

1. Change your view to agree with theirs; for example, you
   can concur with Newton's assertion that kids who never
   do any homework are more likely to become Nobel Prize
   winners.
2. Hold on to your opinion but don't argue with theirs;
   in other words, stop talking the instant you sense an
   argument shaping up.

Agreeing with teens doesn't necessarily mean you have to ignore
reality. Sometimes agreement is your best option.

OXFORD: If I have to wait until my grades come up to get
a driver's license, I might as well just buy a bike
now.

YOU: I was thinking that too.

ELVIS: If I turn my music down any more, I might as well
turn it off.

YOU: That'd be nice.

No sarcasm or patronizing. You're simply acknowledging Oral's opinion, but you're not backing away from yours. Oxford may indeed have to put thirty-two thousand miles on his bike before he decides to change academic gears.

Trying to convince kids with reason, especially while they're being highly unreasonable, is to get pulled into a verbal black hole. For every point you make, they'll counter with two. "Music nowadays is meant to be played loud. Your music was written for the old days, when times were quieter." Now I ask, how can you dispute such logic?

One savvy response is the closed-mouth move. Give Polly a gaze that says, "I'm not wrangling any further." A look speaks much.

Winning an argument with Victor means getting him to acknowledge begrudgingly that your perspective has at least one molecule of merit, if only among other old folks. Only as I moved into my twenties did my parents and I begin to look at the world through shared eyes. And I'll admit that was a bit scary for me because they hadn't gotten any cooler.

---

Only as I moved into my twenties
did my parents and I begin to look
at the world through shared eyes. And
I'll admit that was a bit scary for me
because they hadn't gotten any cooler.

---

Other ways to pull out when staying in is going nowhere:

Walk away calmly. Some kids will let you leave the scene and not follow you out to the car, pleading, "Mom, just wait; one more thing," as you lock the door and crank up the radio.

To reach for elite parenthood, master the "dumb look," an expression that face-wise conveys, "Not only am I not going to argue, but I don't even understand what we're arguing about." The look is highly effective against flawless illogic like "Why should I study? The more I know, the more I forget. And the more I forget, the less I know. So why study?" If a teen thinks our brain is skidding, we might as well play the role to our advantage.

One mom told me that the dumb look seemed to her like a smart idea. But she sometimes naturally felt dumb around the kids, and she wasn't sure they'd know when she was giving that look or just being herself. I didn't know how to answer her, so I just gave her a dumb look.

# Too Much Reasoning Is Illogical

*Dear Dr. Ray,*

*The more I give my children my reasons, the more they ask why. Should I keep repeating my reasons?*

*Out of Answers*

Why? Give me one good reason why you should.

Kids are real child psychologists. When we ask Kitty why she threw the cat onto the roof, invariably we hear, "I don't know." But when she repeatedly badgers us as to why she can't play with Sylvester anymore today, we feel obliged to offer fifteen answers in the vain hope of hitting on one she'll accept.

Giving kids our reasons is wise practice. It reveals the method to our madness and that we're not bucking for the "Tyrant Parent of the Decade" award. We actually do have a rationale for wanting the trash hauled out before the bacteria multiply enough to eat a hole in the bag.

Giving kids our reasons becomes unwise—not to mention nerve-racking—when we're doing nothing but repeating ourselves. Who hasn't, in total exasperation, finally bellowed, "Because I'm your mother, that's why!" or, "Because I said so!" or the time-tested, "Because!"? Firing off these lines, we shuddered to hear ourselves sounding just like our own parents. As children, we promised aloud, "I'll never say that to my kids." What we didn't realize then and what our own youngsters don't realize now is that kids can receive fifteen logical answers as to why curfew can't be 2:00 a.m., each of which they will counter until Mom or Dad, hitting the limits of human endurance, explodes with "Because I said so!"

No doubt you've reviewed for Ripley the reasons behind your rules and requirements dozens, maybe hundreds, of times, and he was still a preschooler. It's not that he doesn't believe or understand them. He just doesn't agree with or like or appreciate them. Can you expect him to? He's a kid. If he agreed with all your parenting, he wouldn't need you to raise him. He could raise himself.

If Sherlock asks you more than once—okay, twice—why he can't stay overnight at Watson's house, he's telling you he's not really interested in knowing why. He wants to debate. His motto: "Keep Mom repeating herself until she wears down." Have you ever answered multiple whys or why nots and, on number fourteen, seen Sherlock's face light up? "Gosh, Mom. I've been so difficult. Thank you for explaining it to me. That last one did it."

So do you provide your reasons? Yes—once, or maybe twice if you suspect you weren't heard the first time around. More than that, is just begging for an argument. You could say, "I gave you my reason. You didn't like it" and then say no more. Or use the sound bite "What part of no don't you understand?"

On complex issues such as smoking or driving privileges, discussions are helpful. But on most day-to-day matters, you've no doubt explained yourself ragged. Why drag through the same ritual each and every time it's Madge's turn to clear the table or Taylor has to put his jacket in the closet instead of over the sink? Here no explanations are called for; discipline is.

# If at First You Don't Succeed

*Dear Dr. Ray,*

*Just when I think I'm handling a situation well, it blows up.*

*Shell-Shocked*

Some years ago, I was playing in a softball tournament. A five-year-old boy walked up behind me and, with his bat, took a few swings at my legs. Since I'm allergic to aluminum smacking my body at forty miles an hour—I break out in red welts—I corrected the young Babe, "Okay, that's enough. Can it." Can you hear my professional training?

My teammates immediately started swinging. "Mr. Psycho-man knows kids. 'Can it.' He's too smooth."

To prove that I am no rinky-dink shrink, I rushed to my car and grabbed my Psychology 605 textbook, a thick tome on how to handle any kid, anywhere, anytime. (The book is always in my trunk. One never knows when an emergency roadside healing will be necessary.) After memorizing the section on bat-wielding five-year-olds, I returned ready to reassert my skills.

First, I bent down the little guy's eye level. As veterinarians recommend, "Don't tower over a wild animal. Lower your threat profile." Next came an expression of feelings: "I don't like being hit with a ball bat." Translation: I'm not comfortable with where your bat is coming from. I can't go with that.

Then I went with natural consequences: "If you swing at me, I'll just walk away." Message: You swing, no target, no game, no fun.

While speaking soothingly, I slowly guided his bat to the ground. After all, keeping my verbal and nonverbal cues in sync is critical. Otherwise, I'd be sending mixed messages.

Finally, my coup de bat. "Please put the bat down, and we'll play catch with my softball." Call it an informal contingency contract, with a variable ratio reinforcement schedule for maximum response effectiveness. In one thirty-seven-second mini speech, I covered about five therapeutic approaches. This little scamp was set to be putty in my hands.

All I can assume is that he didn't read my Psych 605 textbook. No sooner had I finished than he finished: "Yeah, right. Get real, Jerk Face."

I should have stuck with "Can it," though I did learn a hard-hitting lesson: Don't be quick to grade your technique after one try. If a child is involved, two other variables are too: unpredictability and time—lots of both.

When you're convinced you're handling trouble well—staying calm, reasonable, resolute—most likely you are. That doesn't guarantee all will end smoothly. Kids are not consistently rational creatures (who is?), particularly when being disciplined. So your maturity doesn't guarantee their maturity.

---

When you're convinced you're
handling trouble well—staying calm,
reasonable, resolute—most likely you are.
That doesn't guarantee all will end smoothly.

---

The first few times you're calmly firm, you may not be rewarded. It is the cumulative effect over time that brings success.

That's probably why, after my professionally choreographed monologue, I didn't hear, "Why, thank you, sir. I most certainly am sorry for swinging at you. Please accept my apology, and I would love to interact with you and the softball in a mutually satisfactory way."

Actually, I think I would have been more shocked had I heard this than "Yeah, right ..."

# Perfectly Reasonable

*Dear Dr. Ray,*

*My daughter, age sixteen, accuses, "You expect me to be perfect," if I discipline her or put limits on her freedom.*

*Imperfect Parent*

Well, *do* you expect her to be perfect? I would hope so. Any expectation for responsible and moral conduct comes with an ideal to strive toward. Disciplining your daughter for disrespect conveys that you expect respect—all the time, not just some of the time. Grounding her for ignoring curfew reinforces that your curfew rules are in place every night, not just Tuesdays and the second Thursday following a full moon.

Most likely, your daughter is not actually accusing you of expecting perfection; she is complaining about rules she doesn't like. She may be labeling your standards "perfect" when she really means "too high, in my opinion." For instance, if you punish her for mistreating a sibling, she concludes you're not allowing her to make a mistake or to act badly—in other words, to be human. If you were being reasonable, you'd understand that the best of people do wrong things, and you'd give her some room to do wrong.

Indeed, you are being reasonable, perfectly so. To expect perfect behavior is not to expect someone to be perfect. It is to establish a standard to teach by.

I wanted my kids' rooms orderly. Were they? What do you think? Even as I enforced my room rules, I knew that the rooms would never be kept to my liking, much less perfectly so. This does not mean that I didn't hold to some kind of ideal. Further, my standard was, in fact, not all that high, but compared with my kids' standard, it was in the stratosphere.

> To expect perfect behavior is not to expect someone to be perfect. It is to establish a standard to teach by.

Then too, if your daughter's idea of good conduct is lower than yours—and I'll bet it is—then she's branding you a perfectionist not because you are but because you expect more of her than she does. Which means, in her opinion, your standards are not just higher than hers but higher than most anybody's. Teens have a proclivity for seeing their way as the only reasonable way.

When was the last time your daughter thought you eminently fair for disciplining her? Yesterday? Last year? When she was three? It is a truth of life that kids—and most adults—can justify their behavior enough to excuse it from any consequences. If another person, especially one in authority, doesn't agree with their thinking, he or she is being intolerant of fallible human nature.

Can you use my arguments on your daughter? Are you kidding? What are you, a perfectionist? You can use them on yourself, though, to feel less guilty and vulnerable to your daughter's perception.

When will your daughter come to appreciate your so-called perfectionism? When she's paying her own bills? When she has teenagers? When she's perfect?

There is irony to all this. Your daughter sees your standards as demanding perfection. What she doesn't see is that these standards are what are making her a better person. Along with that, she'll come to see how far we all are from perfection.

# So Did You

*Dear Dr. Ray,*

*How do I respond to an adolescent boy who, upon being disciplined, says, "You did the same things when you were my age"?*

*Dumber Then*

How did your son know you did the same things when you were his age? Who told him? Whoever it was has made your parenting tougher. There is a point where communication from parent—or grandparent—to child can be too open.

Since he now knows, don't provide any more details. Your past, however wrong or stupid, is not his concern unless you wish it to be. But remember, whatever you say can and may be held against you.

Your moral authority as a parent does not depend one whit upon your moral conduct as a child. If it did, few of us could claim clean parental status. The process of maturing dictates that we are more foolish and shortsighted when younger. However you wish to convey this to your son, do so. But don't expect him to understand or agree. That's part of his immaturity.

> Your moral authority as a parent does not depend one whit upon your moral conduct as a child.

Next, admit that you were once a child. "You're right. I did teenager things when I was a teenager." Keep admissions deliberately vague. Even though you refuse to be manipulated, no sense giving your son more fodder about your past to chew on.

Point three: Contrary to what your son thinks, you are not so fossilized to recall only hazily what impulses, desires, and dangers accompany youth. It is your memory of having been his age that makes you acutely aware of how to help him safely navigate his age now. Part of being a good parent is knowing the reality of being bad as a kid.

Now, your masterstroke. With no shame, inform your son how lucky he is that you, too, once did wrong things — though not anymore, of course. It is your own youthful misconduct that is helping you to be the vigilant parent you are today. Through firsthand back-then experience, you understand how critical it is to protect him from potential foolishness and discipline him for actual foolishness. Whatever you might have once gotten away with was not to your benefit.

You could also say, "You're right. I did do some dumb things when I was your age. But now my job is to raise the best person I can. And that means raising someone who is better than I was."

Not much bugs a teen more than when a parent compliments at the same time she sets limits.

3

# More Authority = Less Discipline

Parenthood is packed with irony. During the teen years, parents need to be at their child-rearing strongest. The typical teen is more savvy and willful than even the feistiest preschooler. And discipline decisions are much more complex than ferreting out who kicked over Mason's toy blocks.

This phase, though, is when many parents' discipline stamina is waning. We've been at this for at least twelve years. Just when we're hoping to ease up on our guidance, discipline, and supervision, we're pushed to ramp up all three.

If we don't have quite the energy and stamina we had when younger, we'd best find some ways to compensate. Calm, confident authority is a key way. It's an inverse relationship: The better your authority, the less you have to discipline.

# Better Late Than Never

*Dear Dr. Ray,*

My son is fifteen. I've been a weak disciplinarian since he was small. Is it too late to change, for his sake and mine?

*Slow Learner Mom*

It's too late to change when this life is over. Until then, forward movement is always possible. It may come only by the inch. Still, the inches are in the right direction.

Your doctor discovers that you've been eating foods damaging to your stomach. What would you do? Would you stop eating those foods immediately, even if unsure your stomach would settle? At the least, you want no further damage; at best, you want to heal.

At some point, many parents become aware of heading in a frustrating direction. The signs accumulate. That awareness doesn't always lead to change. But for those for whom it does, there is bad news and good news. The bad news: The longer the wrong direction, the slower and harder to reverse it. The good news: Now that the direction is reversed, the more likely a good outcome.

Once you start to change, how will your son change? In behavior first; in his attitude later.

Suppose you establish a new house rule: All chores and duties (including schoolwork) must be completed before any privileges begin. Your son—once he comes to believe that this new you is really you and not some alien life force controlling his mother's body—should start to comply within weeks, maybe days, though only because he is feeling forced and only because it is in his self-interest.

For a little while, your son will be convinced more than ever that you are unreasonable, dictatorial, or arbitrary—and these are your better qualities. Such is standard course. Actions reverse more quickly than minds. Many of your son's unruly ways are years old. They won't be fixed in two months.

---

## Actions reverse more quickly than minds.

---

When will his attitude improve? I don't know (I get paid for this). But I do know that if you persevere through his resistance, teeth-gritting compliance may evolve into respectful cooperation.

There are further reasons to reverse your parenting. And their number corresponds exactly to the number of younger siblings. They are watching closely what you are allowing Big Brother. Change your direction now, and you will change theirs too. And you won't have to ask "Is it too late?" again.

# Reversing Directions

*Dear Dr. Ray,*

*I've been a lax disciplinarian for years. Should I change all at once or gradually?*

*Coming to My Senses*

Change all at once. That's the best way. Even so, you will change only gradually. Your parenting style and habits have the momentum of several years. Suddenly slamming on the brakes and reversing engines won't result in an immediate 180-degree turnabout. Most likely, you'll skid for a while, creep to a halt, and then slowly change old habits.

Turning around a large ship in the ocean takes up to twelve miles. And that's a ship without kids. You're not the size of a ship, but you're far more complex. Altering a ship's course is child's play compared with altering a parenting course.

> Altering a ship's course is child's play
> compared with altering
> a parenting course.

Nevertheless, adjust your ways, and with full speed ahead. First, the longer you delay, the longer bad habits have to harden further. Shedding bad habits a little at a time is like trying to quit smoking a little at a time. You're struggling to conquer the very behavior in which you keep indulging.

Second, gradual change leads to erratic change. To illustrate, this month, you'll tackle the big three: back talk, defiance, and sibling quibbling. Next month, you'll work on clothes debris, phone excess, and ignored chores. Suppose, at the end of month, the big three are still present. Do you allot them another month while ignoring the "lesser" troubles? And when is a particular problem conquered? At 50 percent less? 75 percent? In fact, most misbehavior never completely goes away. So if you wait until one problem is no more, you'll never address any others.

Third, the forms of misconduct overlap. For example, back talk and defiance may be intertwined with phone misuse. Sibling quibbling can mix with chore hassles. You can't isolate one problem without simultaneously incorporating others.

Fourth, misconduct needs to be stopped fast. When you sense you're drinking spoiled milk, do you swallow more slowly or spit it out? If your child were acting poorly, would you allow him three months to give it up?

How will your kids react to the new you? They'll be shell-shocked. Who is this stranger? Whose book has she been reading? How long until she gets back to her old ways?

Kids don't always realize what is good for them, so they resist it. Nevertheless, they'll have to accept the fact that this better parent is here to stay and will only get better. And they'll change, too, into more cooperative children who'll come to accept, even appreciate, the way things have changed.

# Pendulum Parenting

*Dear Dr. Ray,*

*As a teenager, I experienced harsh and erratic discipline. I'm so afraid of doing the same to my kids (ages fourteen and fifteen) that I tend toward being permissive and lax.*

*Overcompensator*

The opposite of harsh is not permissive; it is lovingly strong. The opposite of erratic is not lax; it is consistent.

The drive to parent opposite from one's own harsh or hurtful upbringing is a strong one. Long-ago emotions may reverberate, evoking disturbing memories of feeling misunderstood and mistreated. Consequently, to make sure that you don't provoke similar feelings in your kids, you scrupulously seek to avoid disagreement or conflict. The primary goal of your parenting is peace, even when your better judgment says to stand your ground when facing friction.

There are two traps lurking in this mindset. One, it is not possible to avoid upsetting kids. Socializing a child means making innumerable decisions that he will find disagreeable, unfair, arbitrary, or "mean." And at times, he will see you as disagreeable, unfair, arbitrary, or "mean." Good parents are ready to "cause" in their children some *temporary*—that is the operative word—feelings of being misunderstood or mistreated. Otherwise, they'll decide for themselves how to run their own lives, at ages fourteen and fifteen.

Two, even if, for the moment, you can sidestep conflict, over the years more conflict will arise. It's just not possible to parent in a way your kids will always find fair and agreeable. More of your decisions, no matter how compromising, will anger them.

Core Law of Human Nature Number 103: You can't satisfy others—big or little—by yielding to their every desire. They will more quickly react to the slightest whiff that you are not doing things as they wish.

The final irony? The very thing you so desperately want to avoid —a harsh and erratic relationship with your children—you risk inviting. They won't appreciate your lax parenting, as they want more and more laxness in order to be pacified. At the same time, you'll fight frustration and impotence, as no matter how much you try to get along, you won't get credit for it.

So how to avoid this spiraling cycle?

First, the opposite of harsh parenting is confident parenting. It is calm, loving resolve. To be firm is not mean or dictatorial. It is doing well by your children—now and in the future.

> The opposite of harsh parenting
> is confident parenting.
> It is calm, loving resolve.

Second, your kids' unreasonable reaction to your limits and rules does not automatically indicate that you are being unreasonable. There is a major difference between unfair discipline and discipline that kids think is unfair. In loving homes, a teen's bad reaction to rules is not usually a reliable indicator that the rules are bad.

Finally, in all likelihood, your parents didn't give much thought to their ways and their effects on you. They did what they did, for better or worse. That you are so concerned about your behavior reflects a desire to be a better parent than you knew. This is pretty solid evidence that your style is not harsh or erratic. Indeed, one way to risk being harsh is to be so afraid of acting firm that you don't allow yourself to do so.

# It's Only a Stage

*Dear Dr. Ray,*

*I've realized that I need to take firmer discipline stands with my kids, but they don't seem to be taking me seriously. It's as though they're just waiting for me to go back to my old self.*

*A New Woman, Really*

They are. Kids are natural-born skeptics, at least where discipline is concerned. They will settle for nothing less than time and consistency from us before being convinced that our new resolve is for real.

Wise parents make adjustments, sometimes big ones. Routinely a mother or father will contact me, spurred on by the realization that "something has to change" in the home. The kids have become the heads of the household, and the parents are hostages to increasing misbehavior. (Is "misbehavior" a politically incorrect child-rearing term? Is an expert somewhere intoning, "There is no misbehavior, only misunderstood behavior"?)

> The kids have become the heads of the household, and the parents are hostages to increasing misbehavior.

Generally, the younger a child is when a parent decides that setting limits is not "tough love" but *is* love, the less bumpy the road back to a parent-centered household. Too many parents are mistreated for ten to fifteen years before realizing they've let their authority slip away. Life then becomes the child's teacher, forcing lessons far more roughly than Mom or Dad ever did.

Your insight carries two commitments: (1) to maintain and boost your newfound determination and (2) to convince your kids that this reborn mother is just the beginning. Fortunately, if you do the first, the second will take care of itself.

As you know, kids aren't inclined to take the new you seriously. "What is this? Did you see some shrink on TV today, Mom?" "Did you go buy some new parenting book?" After speaking with me a few times, parents tell me their kids ask, "Who have you been talking to?"

Is this an insult? Meaning you aren't capable of changing yourself on our own. There must be some influence somewhere prodding you to be more self-assured, and once it's gone, your spine will return to Styrofoam.

You could play with your kids' heads a bit. Tape a copy of this page to the refrigerator. They'll think it's the source of your confidence. If it mysteriously disappears in an hour, tape up another. If that is swiped, your kids will relax, thinking your phase is about to pass now that the shrink's words have been erased, only to find your resolve is internal and not taped to a door.

Who can blame kids when doubting discipline resolve? Regularly, parents "have had it up to here" and promise that "there are going to be some changes around here, young man." Whereupon Bruno lowers his unruly profile awhile until the status quo returns. This cycle trims a little credibility each time we start it and don't live it through. So when you've finally, really, truly, actually had enough, be prepared to prove it for a long time—in fact, for the rest of their childhood.

## Standing Strong

You could tell your kids, "You know, you guys are right. This is a phase I'm going through. It will be about fifteen years long." Or until they move out, whichever comes first.

# The Authority Test

*Dear Dr. Ray,*

*I used to think I was a pretty strong parent, but I'm beginning to wonder. As my children have gotten older, they're resisting my discipline with more intensity.*

*Shaky Mom*

Here's a brief test of parental authority. Next time your child does something wrong or bad—

Wait. Can we still use words like *bad* and *wrong*? In our value-neutral culture, must we morally antisepticize the language, as some experts assert? "Blade, putting the ice pick in your sister's foot is inappropriate conduct." No, it's really bad conduct. Just ask his sister.

Next time your youngster acts badly or wrongly, do a field experiment. In a calm tone of voice, one time, levy a consequence: "Eve, you are being very disrespectful. Head for your room; your night is over." "I asked you three times to clean the bathroom, Hazel. You ignored me all three times. You now have an hour of new chores. Let's begin immediately." "Webster, you will write a four-hundred-word apology to your teacher for being disruptive in her class." "Because you called your little brother a name, Forbes, you will pay him two dollars."

Then observe what happens. Is there cooperation? Disbelief? Negotiation? Argument? A look saying, "I'll comply, but you and everybody else will pay for the next six hours"? Is there stomping? outright refusal?

In short, how does your child react? This reveals how he views your authority. A child's response to discipline is influenced more by his perception of his parent than by his temperament.

> A child's response to discipline
> is influenced more by his
> perception of his parent
> than by his temperament.

Far too many children are labeled strong-willed who are not. Their conduct may look strong-willed, but, in fact, it is emboldened by their perception of Mom or Dad as weak-willed. The more a youngster believes a parent's discipline is questionable or challengeable, the stronger his will to resist it.

So how do parents score on the authority test? My forty years of results say that the average American parent with the average American child does not get cooperation without at least some resistance, sometimes heavy. If, by nature, Butkus is easy or mature or compliant, then he usually cooperates with discipline more or less on his own. But if he is normal-natured or a bit stronger, getting resistance is more common than acceptance for many moms and dads.

How did you do? What did your kids do? There is good news and bad news. The bad news: If the kids resisted, in word or deed, you can conclude pretty safely that they don't see you as having legitimate authority. The good news: You can change this perception by changing yourself.

A generation or two ago, more parents would have passed the test. Again, perception. Kids viewed parents—indeed, most grown-ups—as having authority. That's because the grown-ups also viewed themselves so and acted accordingly. The irony is that if a parent has authority in a child's mind, she doesn't have to assert it often; it's a given. If she doesn't have authority in the child's mind, she has to try to assert some weaker form of it, usually with words or emotion.

So how do you begin to change a child's perception and thus re-establish yourself as a confident parent? Allow my wife to illustrate.

Some years back, my son Andrew asked, "Mom, what would you do if you told me to do something and I just refused?" At age fifteen, a weightlifter and feeling a bit like a young stallion, he knew he was now physically the second-strongest person in the house. (His twelve-year-old sister was first.)

My wife's response: "Andrew, I'd have to shut you down. All of your privileges, activities, favorite foods, and electronic goodies would cease until you cooperate."

Andrew's counter: "But what if you did all that and I just walked out?"

Randi's move, checkmate: "Oh, that's different. Then I would do two things. First, I'd cry because I love you so much. Then I would blow my nose and call the police."

"Mom, you know I wouldn't do anything like that." But if he did, she would call because she does love him that much and because she will not permit a child to so deliberately defy her authority.

I suggest to parents a technique called "blackout." Suppose you assign your daughter, for her nasty tone, a two-hundred-word essay on respect. She reacts with some version of "Yeah, right. Like I'm going to do that." You now have two options.

One, find another consequence she'll accept.

Good luck.

Two, show her that you are ready to stand even stronger. Implement blackout. Blackout is immediate cessation of all perks and privileges—except love, food and, okay, the bathroom—until you get your initial consequence.

How will Bliss get to soccer practice? All her transportation is shut down until you get the essay—which is now longer, as she refused the original. She has no phone to call anyone for a ride or to text friends about her plight. She can't even go to neighbors for help, as she's not allowed outside. There are no other activities except school, reading, and chores.

Gone, too, are the television, radio, and computer. If she uses any possessions of entertainment, they are taken—for a time or for good, your call. As for school, Bliss has to pack her own lunch, as there is no money supply; it, too, is shut off. Even eating out is a privilege, so while Bliss must go along, she eats at home before you all leave.

All kids misbehave—lots. But when a child blatantly refuses to accept legitimate discipline, he has dramatically intensified his resistance. Here a parent has to be at her most resolute. Blackout is one way to convey the fact that you see defiance as a major misbehavior and will respond accordingly.

# Red Corvette Discipline

*Dear Dr. Ray,*

*What do you think when a parent says, "I can't wait until he can drive. Then I'll have something to hang over his head to make him cooperate"?*

*Automatic*

I'd think, "Well, buy him a red Corvette when he turns sixteen, and then you'll have something really cool to hang over his head."

Alas, not even a red Corvette can get cooperation when past discipline has been shaky.

First, if a parent hopes for future privileges to make discipline work, what does that say about his discipline now? The more authority a parent has let slip away, the less likely removing new privileges, however prized, will evoke much cooperation. In fact, such discipline is likely to bring on more conflict, as Carson gets really mad if Mom messes with something as treasured as the car keys. If, in his eyes, she had no past right to take away his stuff, why would she have any present right, especially now that he's older?

Second, even if Carson does become more pleasant, what is his motive? Is it solely to maintain license rights? If holding on to one big privilege is the driving force behind treating his parents well, what happens if he loses that privilege? What big stick is left to Mom or Dad? Healthy authority is never founded upon one or two consequences, no matter how potent they might be.

Healthy authority is never founded
upon one or two consequences, no
matter how potent they might be.

Third, discipline teaches quicker when it removes more than just excess. Many teens' existence is a mini Disney World. So if Mickey gets mouthy and loses his Xbox, no big deal. Still untouched is the computer, TV, stereo, four-wheeler, semiannual cruise, and beach home in Florida. When a child is "disciplined" by having 8 percent of a 97 percent inventory removed, he won't learn much; while driving might be a big-ticket item, it is still taking away only part of way too much anyway.

Fourth, driving is a privilege to be earned, not an entitlement of age, as most kids, even many parents, believe. The guiding question is "Has Ford shown himself mature enough to deserve wheels under him?" If a parent is counting on a car to be the ultimate discipline leverage, the question has been answered: Carson is not ready to drive. There is no reason even to consider "having something to hang over his head" because he doesn't deserve having that something in the first place.

When a child is responsible with present privileges, a parent can then contemplate adding new ones. It is seldom wise to provide new perks when the old ones haven't yet taught responsibility.

# No More Room

*Dear Dr. Ray,*

*I've heard, "Don't send children to their rooms for punishment. It pairs something negative with someplace that should be positive."*

*Where to Now?*

I must be conflicted and don't realize it. I was sent to my room regularly growing up. Whatever "bad room feelings" I developed were either repressed—until I uncover them on some future visit to a TV talk show—or else subdued by all the good feelings triggered by sleep, privacy, reading, and naps.

Indeed, I have yet to meet any adult traumatized or even queasy over living through involuntary room punishment in childhood. You'd think I'd bump into a few with residual room angst as a small part of their adult troubles.

> I have yet to meet any adult traumatized or even queasy over living through involuntary room punishment in childhood.

This is Child-Rearing Cliché Number 27. It is one of many "enlightened" corrections on traditional discipline: Spanking breeds aggression; corners are humiliating; time-out is isolating; writing apologies breeds distaste for English; a money fine breaks trust, as it retracts a committed allowance.

Is anything still psychologically okay to use? How about taking away privileges or possessions? Well, that depends, goes the argument. Are they gifts from another person? Did Penny pay for them herself? Are they related to the crime? How long will they be taken? Was Penny sufficiently warned?

Most any discipline consequence has many other uses. I like chairs. I'm sitting on one now. Do I want to sit on one facing a corner? No, that's boring.

I'm writing presently, making money doing so. Do I want to be forced to write something about my misbehavior on my own time—for free? Nope.

I use rulers to measure things. They're handy for household repairs. Was a ruler used to measure my behind a few times as a kid? Yep. Am I afraid of rulers now? Not at all, unless they're career politicians.

Most places and things can be good or bad, helpful or hurtful, depending upon the context in which they occur. Further, except in extreme cases, contexts don't overlap. One doesn't color the other. Involuntary room time doesn't spoil voluntary room time.

Much of what makes discipline effective is lack of choice. If Nielsen happens to be too busy to watch TV for two days, he doesn't feel deprived. It's his decision. If you suspend his TV for two days, he does feel deprived.

If Knap retreats to his bed for a two-hour snooze, he's content. If you send him to bed two hours early, he's discontent. Time, place, and freedom make all the difference in seeing something as reward or as punishment.

Try an exercise. Next time Butkus acts up, give him a choice: He can either wash the car or go to his room for an hour. See which he prefers. See if he's pleased to be given options. And see if his room isn't chosen. It's all in the timing.

# Lengthening Your Fuse

*Dear Dr. Ray,*

*How can I discipline my children without getting angry? I find myself becoming easily frustrated with my sons, ages nine and thirteen.*

*Trip Switch*

There's big pressure on parents these days to practice 100 percent anger-free discipline. Resist the pressure; it can't be done. No parent disciplines without getting angry sometimes.

I do recall one first-time mom who determined to stay calm from day one. She was hospitalized with stomach distress, but her sixteen-month-old was allowed to visit her.

Anytime our emotions are wrapped tightly around another human being, we will act wrongly, such as saying regrettable words, losing control, and yelling. Emotions, even negative ones, are signs of close correction. This said, most of us admit we could do a calmer job of child raising and, in particular, disciplining.

Ponder the parenting debut. On day one, we are blessed with a being with zero social skills. It is absolutely self-absorbed. It wants what it wants the nanosecond it wants it, becoming a raving lunatic if it doesn't get it.

Over the better part of the next two decades, we strive to permeate this being with self-control, maturity, and morals. Along the way, we face thousands of pieces of resistant, obnoxious, difficult, thoughtless, moody, selfish behavior. This isn't a negative picture. It's reality. And lest thousands seem an exaggeration, if a youngster misbehaves only once per day (let me study this angel), in sixteen years, the total is over five thousand.

---

If a youngster misbehaves only
once per day (let me study this angel),
in sixteen years the total
is over five thousand.

---

Most parents grasp this reality intellectually but forget it emotionally. But accepting it when it presents itself daily—hourly?—will ease frustration. This is not to say tolerate or overlook misconduct, but just knowing it's an inescapable part of raising any child will help us react to misconduct more evenhandedly.

One definition of stress is "the difference between the way we'd like things to be and the way that they are." Should we picture a Hallmark-card family scene with an ever-cooperative Chastity and Oxford walking with us, we will in exasperation wonder, "What's wrong?" When kids misbehave, most of the time, nothing is wrong. They're acting like kids, and they're making us act like parents.

Nonetheless, there are techniques to help us be calmer parents.

*Act early in the chain.* Butkus ignores, defies, or debates. Parent repeats, prods, argues, threatens. Butkus resists louder, talks tougher, escalates. Parent stands ground, gets upset, disciplines. The whole scenario takes twenty-seven minutes to unfold. By the time Mom or Dad acts, words have multiplied and emotions have flared. Who wouldn't be agitated at that point?

Don't allow the scenario to get on a roll. Discipline early, before your cool evaporates. Butkus will likely accept his discipline better.

*Get out of each other's faces, separating for a while.* As soon as you feel your temperature rising, think about sending Butkus to his room, or go to yours. You can address the trouble when you're back to 98.6 degrees. Distance is a great sedative. It helps clear minds and soften words.

*Delay.* If a problem or misbehavior is baffling or worrisome, it doesn't always need to be fixed instantly. Time between your discovery and your response to the misconduct, like distance, settles emotions—maybe not completely but enough to balance them with reason.

*Lower your voice.* John Wayne's acting advice is sound advice for parents: Talk low, talk slow. Force yourself to speak more deliberately even as you feel less deliberate. Lower volume can temper a fiery reaction.

The relationship between emotions and behavior is two-directional. Emotions lead to action—for better or worse—but actions can alter emotions. When you don't feel calm, act calm. Fake it if you have to. At the least, your kids will wonder what's wrong with you. Maybe you snapped, and now who knows what kind of discipline you'll concoct. Low and slow talk is not only more credible; it gets more attention.

No parent can be calm all the time. Nor would you want to be. Upset can make a definite statement. The problem comes when upset rules too often.

Our level of frustration is not linked solely to our kids' conduct. We can raise or lower our exasperation through our style. We are not emotional pawns to our children's behavior: They act bad; we get mad. In fact, our behavior influences theirs more than theirs does ours. We change, and they will. That's the aim anyway.

# Time to Work

*Dear Dr. Ray,*

*How about some ideas for discipline that works?*

*Impatient*

It depends on what you mean by "works." Almost all discipline works immediately: It teaches a lesson. It says to Sherlock, "If you do A, I'll do B." Elementary.

This is not, however, what most people mean by "discipline that works." They mean discipline that improves Watson's behavior for the better—and fast. The aim is desirable, but it often leads to undesirable outcomes. It can cause pinball parenting, bouncing from approach to approach, scouring for that one to cure instantly the maddeningly repetitive misconduct.

"I've tried everything; nothing works. I have talked until hoarse, taken away his favorite game until 2056, applied seventeen different reward systems, promised an all-expenses-paid trip to Disney World, threatened grounding with backup banishment to Siberia. Finally, I got totally frustrated. I sent him on an errand to the neighbor's and moved while he was gone."

As parents list all they've tried—and, in their minds, fruit-lessly—I find that they actually tried plenty that would have worked, given enough time. They assumed that if they didn't see quick re-sults, they were on the wrong track. Not necessarily. The discipline was working—just not as soon as they had hoped or expected.

Don't different kids respond differently to different discipline? Sure. Macy would do absolutely anything to avoid losing her favorite sweatshirt for a week, while Levi doesn't know the difference between a sweatshirt and sweat socks. On the other hand, Levi sweat bullets over writing, "I will treat my sister better" twenty-five times. Discipline "works" at different speeds for some kids than others, but almost all discipline needs more time to change a child's behavior than grown-ups would like. Such is the nature of discipline and kids.

Am I trying to weasel out of answering your question? Well, whatever works. Okay, here are a few ideas for making discipline work faster.

1. *Keep it simple.* Repetition is what makes discipline succeed. And it's hard to persevere with complicated consequences. Pick those you can use for daily trouble: corner time, monetary fines, extra chores, writing sentences or essays, room time, remodeling the attic (not all at once). Be ready to "repeat as necessary."

2. *Be patient.* God gives most of us decades to improve ourselves. We can give the kids a few years to improve themselves. Discipline is a process, not a fix.

> Discipline is a process, not a fix.

3. *Stay the course.* Almost any reasonable consequence will work—that is, change the behavior—given enough perseverance. I know, you'd like to retire in thirty-one years. Nonetheless, time is your ally. Good, steady discipline does teach good behavior, even while your child is still in childhood.

# A Lifetime of Discipline

*Dear Dr. Ray,*

*I think I'm pretty consistent in my discipline, yet my son (age thirteen) still gets into trouble for the same things again and again. Why is it taking so long?*

*Waiting*

Kids repel discipline. Being held accountable for their actions is not high on their song list of "My Favorite Things." Conventional child-rearing notions say, "Children want discipline. They want the security of knowing there are rules and limits to live by." Yes, when they're years older and can look back: "Now I understand why my parents (teachers, grandpa, aunt) did what they did."

But right as it's happening—at the moment of feeling its consequences—discipline is not something Frank wants. Have you ever overheard Frank telling his friend, "Hey, Igor, why don't you come over to my house and let my mom discipline us awhile? She's pretty good at it."

Far enough removed from on-the-spot discipline, kids may see its value and even be grateful here and there. But right as it's about to happen, they'll try to avoid or escape it. And should that be surprising? Children don't understand the why behind most of our parenting. They look at the now and see that we're doing something they see little reason behind.

Has your son ever ventured out of his room after sitting in there for disrespectful talk and said, "Mom, can I talk to you a minute? I was thinking, while I was stuck in my room, watching those guys play football outside without me on probably the last nice day of the year. Oh, yeah, I could have a mom like Lucky's mom. She gives him twenty-five bucks a week for taking out the trash every once in a while. He has a nine-foot TV screen in his bathroom and a wet bar in his closet. I don't have any of that. No, I've got is a mom like you—strict, old-fashioned, doesn't let me get away with much—and I'm grateful.

"You know what else I realized? You're not trying to be mean, are you? You're trying to teach me self-control, and that will help me when I'm all grown up. So if it's all right with you, I'm going to finish my homework and go to bed early, after I clean my room, like you've been nagging."

You'd better check that boy's temperature; he's getting delirious.

If your son agreed with your discipline, if he learned a lesson quickly, would he need you to discipline him? He could probably get by with a consultant who showed up every few months with some recommendations, and he'd take it from there.

> If your son agreed with your discipline …
> would he need you to discipline him?

On the first day of first grade, you could say, "Newton, before you get on the bus, let me tell you something important. Do your arithmetic homework every day for the next twelve years. You don't know what you'll want to do twelve years from now, so keep all your options open, okay?"

And he'd smile, "Why, thank you, Mother. You make so much sense. I'm surprised they never mentioned this in preschool." And you'd never have to monitor his arithmetic homework again.

As much as we grown-ups revere the virtue of owning up to our actions, who of us likes being disciplined? We, too, are inclined to minimize it.

You've just been stopped by a state trooper. "Ma'am, I clocked you at seventy-one miles an hour." Did you correct, "Oh, no, Officer, I was doing at least seventy-six. And yes, you caught me today, but I've been speeding through here every day for the past three years. I should owe the state some back money for that"?

It is the nature of both young and old to avoid unpleasant consequences and thus have to learn things the long way.

# Disciplining for Success

*Dear Dr. Ray,*

*I know discipline needs to be consistent to work best, but it seems I'm on my kids all the time, and I'm not seeing much improvement.*

*Constance*

Consistent discipline does bring results, in time. The key word is *time*, best counted in years, not weeks or months.

Good results often come with the speed of a glacier, not a flash flood. What's more, as slow as we think the kids are to learn, our rate of learning is as much or more glacier-like. Focusing on this reality will help us to answer "Are they ever going to get this?"

Putting discipline in a realistic time frame will lessen your exasperation; it won't eliminate it. Sometimes parents feel as if they are on their kids because they *are* on their kids. Real discipline is being replaced by words and emotions. Nagging, negotiating, pleading, threatening, yelling, chastising, lecturing—all are illusions of discipline. They may sound like discipline, feel like discipline, even get cooperation here and there, but they are not discipline. More and more of the same is needed to get fewer and fewer results.

A self-perpetuating spiral then evolves. Fifty percent of what one is doing fuels the feelings of futility because 50 percent of what one is doing is futile. It is verbal clutter and emotional commotion. Only a small part of what is happening is actual discipline—limits enforced by consequences. Real discipline leads to less discipline over time. Illusory discipline leads to more illusory discipline over time.

Real discipline leads to less discipline over time. Illusory discipline leads to more illusory discipline over time.

To estimate your consistency level, try this exercise. (Brace yourself: The numbers may not be pretty.) Who is your most challenging child, the one who pushes, resists, and frustrates your best parenting efforts? The experts variously would tag this child oppositional, strong-willed, or difficult. Most likely, he is none of these. He is a kid who's feistier by nature than his siblings.

On average, how many times a day does this child ignore you, defy you, erupt, torment a sibling, break a house rule, badger you, slough responsibilities? In other words, how many times a day does he misbehave, as you define it? Parents routinely answer, "Do you want it to the nearest hundred?" or, "The numbers aren't too high at night, but then she's asleep," or, "Let me get my calculator; it goes up to six figures."

After getting down to brass numbers, most totals fall between twenty and fifty. Indeed, twenty is not all that much. If a child is home all day, twenty breaks down to fewer than two incidents per waking hour.

Next question: How many times a day does this child get disciplined—that is, he experiences an actual consequence? Between zero and two is most parents' tally. Those with true Spikes and Spikettes could reach three or four.

Now take the daily discipline average—let's use the high number, say two—and divide that by the low misbehavior number, say twenty. Answer: 10 percent. That is the consistency rate, the percentage of time that a consequence follows misbehavior. Revealing, isn't it?

Of course, I don't know your own consistency numbers. But if your words are substituting for action, that can lead to "I'm on him constantly." A low consistency ratio will dictate that sense.

Sometimes discipline takes a long time to work because a parent takes a long time to discipline. Hunter has been stalking his sister Harmony for the better, or worse, part of an hour. You've ignored, reasoned, and warned, grasping a few seconds' peace for both you and Harmony. Nothing you've tried has brought durable peace (though *durable* often means twelve minutes or more). Finally, you act: "Hunter, you will be your sister's servant for the next hour because you tormented her for an hour." (Marriage prep?)

You did discipline, but you also waited for nearly an hour to do so, allowing plenty of misbehavior during that time. So while Hunter paid the price in the end for his transgressions, he played nearly the whole game for free. For discipline to work well, it must also be timely. The longer a parent waits to discipline, the longer she'll get pulled into illusory discipline.

Good news and bad news. The bad news: The best discipline with the best consistency and the best timing takes longer to shape character than most of us realize. The good news: What is more crucial than shaping character?

# Discipline Discord

*Dear Dr. Ray,*

*My wife and I don't always agree on how to discipline our son and daughter. She says I can be too hard on them. I think she gives in too much.*

*Disunited Front*

Parents who don't always see eye to eye on discipline are the rule rather than the exception. Two people typically don't mesh on something as limited as clothing preference. Can they be expected always to agree on something as involved and evolving as child-rearing?

Parents not sharing one discipline mind is not in itself a deterrent to good parenting. Nor is it necessarily confusing to the children. Its main complication lies in giving the kids the opportunity to play Mom against Dad while listening, gauging the direction of the contest, and aligning with the victor. The victor, in kid parlance, is the parent who most sees things their way.

Nobody wins when parents clash before a youthful audience. Even if one's discipline is more fitting or "correct"—if there always is such a thing—he or she invites other complications, such as broadcasting that Mom and Dad will spar until any discipline is lost in the tangle. If Hector set the folks to bickering—well, worked once, ought to work again. If nothing else, during the confusion he'll be able to quietly slip away.

Should parents never disagree within child earshot? That's not possible. Sometimes both will agree that some discipline is needed, and the give-and-take is just a fine-tuning of the details. Troubles ensue when honest disagreements become undercutting.

To find common discipline ground, talk over incidents later, after they've happened. Agree to disagree, in private, in exchange for mutual alliance at discipline time.

Further, after discussion, should you rethink your initial discipline, an apology is always available. You are not apologizing for disciplining; you are apologizing for your style. A genuine "I'm sorry" does not court inconsistency. Rather, it courts credibility. You are not the rock that never budges.

No matter how diligently you both work to smooth out differences, some will remain. No two parents have identical personalities. They are distinct in patience, tolerance level, voice volume, consistency, and wordiness, among other things. All those translate directly into parenting differences. And that's not always bad. The kids will adjust to where the speed limit is a school zone and where it's the Autobahn.

One sure way to reduce discipline discord is through house rules. These are basic expectations backed by basic consequences. A good house rule has several features:

1. *Both parents agree on it.* Sometimes it's a compromise. Without joint support a house rule becomes another point of child-rearing contention.

2. *A house rule addresses everyday trouble*—back talk, sibling quibbling, chore shirking, or temper tempests. It is suitable for the most irritating and repetitive stuff.

3. *Consequences are clear-cut.* They result automatically when the rule is broken, without nagging (I'm telling you one last time, Butkus, I don't want to have to call in our rule), re-reminding (What did I say was the new rule? Do you remember? Do you want me to write it on

your arm?), or threatening (Okay, break the rule again, and see what happens). Let your consequences do your talking.

4. *Keep rules to a manageable number.* God gave the whole world ten core rules. A house is a much smaller place.

---

God gave the whole world ten core rules.
A house is a much smaller place.

---

With agreed-upon consequences in place, neither of you has to decide what to do each and every time the kids act up. Besides making expectations clearer for the kids, rules make discipline less open-ended for parents.

A sampler of house rules:

1. *You fight, you write.* Each party writes a 250-word apology to the other or others.

2. *You talk back, you walk back,* or *You get mean, you leave the scene.* Back talk leads to an immediate time-out or room time, if logistics permit. If not, delay the room stay until it is convenient. Time doesn't count unless it's quiet time. Or, a 200-word report on a topic of choice researched on the Internet. Who knows, someday they could become *Jeopardy* champions.

3. *Pick up or pay up.* Every item Mom or Dad has to pick up goes into a box (bag, closet, warehouse) for one week. Fifty-cent fee for return.

4. *You shirk, you work.* If you neglect a household chore, privileges are unavailable until that chore and an additional one are completed.

## Standing Strong

Rules are kind discipline for all parties. For kids, rules result in less friction—fewer arguments, harsh words, and hurt feelings. For parents, rules bring peace. In place prior to trouble, they foster order, harmony, and a more united front.

# 4

## Respect Yourself—and Me

Poll a hundred parents of teens: What is your number-one discipline struggle? Survey says: respect. Parents describe disrespect with thesaurus-like variety: attitude, lip, moodiness, mouth, snot. (There's irony in using so many facial terms to describe an age so focused on appearance.)

Something about these adolescent years seems to breed a surge in surliness. Is it to be expected—an immature passage to maturity? Is it something parents have to weather until the kids become nice-talking again? Should you be grateful they're not doing anything worse? After all, they're only misbehaving with words.

Yeah, right. Like no way.

# Battered Parent Syndrome

*Dear Dr. Ray,*

*I'm a grandfather. I'm shocked at how some of my grandkids talk to their parents. And the parents don't even seem to notice.*

*My Father Noticed*

Call it the "Battered Parent Syndrome." Mom or Dad has allowed verbal mistreatment for so long that they have become semi-oblivious to it. The snotty tone, mean retorts, and disdainful looks so penetrate a teen's style that they cease to register.

CHILD: Mom, are you ready to leave yet? What's taking so long? We've been here for over an hour. Let's go.

MOM: I know, Patience. I'm sorry. I'm almost done. Let me finish my coffee, and then we'll go.

CHILD: You said that fifteen minutes ago. If I knew you were going to take this long, I wouldn't have come. Let's go now, not fifteen minutes from now.

MOM: We will. Just give me a few more minutes to finish. Then I'll tell Grandpa goodbye, and I'll be ready to leave.

CHILD: Just hand me the keys. Give me the keys. I'll be in the car. Hurry up.

Patience is blistering her mother, while mom is singing "Kumbaya."

## Patience is blistering her mother, while mom is singing "Kumbaya."

Some parents might accept such surliness as the cost of letting Patience express herself. More often, though, they have habituated to the snarkiness.

Should a "battered parent" scenario erupt in my office, parents may realize something is edgy-sounding, but they can't quite put their finger on what it is. So I ask, "Do you hear how he is talking to you? Is it okay to be treated that way?"

Sometimes the reaction is stunned silence, as if the parent is shaken awake. His look says, "You're right. I am getting mistreated."

Sometimes the reaction is embarrassment. Somebody else has noticed what the parent has been permitting, however unintentionally.

Grandpa, if you're tempted to point out to your children or in-laws what's going on, be careful. They may not only be unaware; they may be defensive. After all, you're pointing out a parenting "flaw." I can broach that more than you can because (1) I'm not a relative, and (2) I'm getting paid to give feedback. Though some folks don't take it so well coming from me either.

You could speak directly to your grandchildren the next time it happens. "Do you hear how you're talking to your father?" Or, "Is that how you speak to your mother?" Your questions are meant for their parents' ears. If your grandchildren were to answer you directly, they might admit, "Yeah, I do," and, "Yes, it is." Of course, if they were so brazen, the shock effect on your children and in-laws might open their ears more than anything you could ever say.

For those of you still raising kids, should you be wondering how much you have slipped into allowing, ask yourself, "How would I react to another adult if he or she spoke to me the way my child is speaking to me?" If your answer is "I'd thank him for being so open and real with his feelings" or "I'd feel flattered that he is so comfortable with our relationship," then you're consistent. You have no problem with young or old talking to you poorly.

If your answer is "I wouldn't like it one bit," then you've opened your eyes—I mean ears. And with your insight, you are now ready to take action to cure the "Battered Parent Syndrome."

# Cutting Back on Back Talk

Dear Dr. Ray,

I have three teenagers, all with distinct personalities. One thing they all have in common, though, is back talk.

*Never the Last Word*

Back talk: a universal teen trait. Unless, that is, Polly absolutely never needs limits or discipline. She just naturally goes to bed before the birds wake up, prefers hanging out with the family, and puts her shoes in the garage before the smoke alarm goes off.

Back talk assumes two types: grumble talk and nasty talk. Grumble talk is the more benign. It is Polly's editorial comment about how you're raising her or running things: "I'm just a servant around here." "How'd you keep the house up before I was born?" "This is the fourth time this week I've had to hang up my coat." "You'd never let me look at you like that; how come Noble gets away with it?"

Grumble talk isn't necessarily disrespectful. It's often more of a whiny "I'm not happy about this." Since it takes two to tangle, if you don't grumble back, most grumble talk ends with a remark or two. You can usually shrug it off, so long as Taylor is hanging up her coat for the fourth time this week or Madge is doing the outlandish work you require.

What can you really say? Fill the dog's water bowl again? How can you drive Duke so hard? Maybe Amber is the only ninth grader in school who has to do her homework before she does her nails.

Grumble talk can be defused through agreement. For instance: "This is the third time I've taken out the garbage this week." "True." Or, "I always have to make my bed." "Yes, you do." No sarcasm. Just a matter-of-fact acknowledgment that what Harmony is grumbling about is the way it is. In effect, you're validating her grumble.

Teens are masters also of the mumble grumble: Turn your back on the closest parent and walk away muttering under your breath, just loud enough to let her know you're saying something but just soft enough so she can't make it out.

According to parent manual, page 69, paragraph B, one response to mumble grumble is "What did you say?" According to teen manual, page 9, subsection C, comebacks are "I didn't say anything" or "Can't a guy even talk to himself around here?" You know he's talking to you; he never talks to himself in that tone.

Two options: One, you can act as if you didn't hear what you sort of heard, using the "prodigal son's brother" principle: If Gladwin is doing what you're asking, he doesn't have to be happy about it. Or two, you can put a price on mumble grumble. Some prices are listed below, under quieting nasty talk.

-------

Using the "prodigal son's brother" principle:
If Gladwin is doing what you're asking,
he doesn't have to be happy about it.

-------

Whereas grumble talk typically doesn't escalate, nasty talk does. Nasty talk is mean or disrespectful, and it directly challenges your parenthood: "Don't tell me what to do." "You're wrong if you think I'm going to do that." "Get off my back." "I don't have to listen to you; just be quiet."

One way to discern nasty talk from grumble talk is to ask, "How would I react to this if it came from another adult?" Nasty talk doesn't keep people friends for very long. Nasty talk is not expressing feelings; it is oral ugliness. And the younger a person is when he's taught to control it, the better for him and others. Nasty talk, if left unchecked, feeds on itself and can become a chronic style.

Nasty talk asks for strong consequences, ones that follow every incident.

1. *Compose an essay on self-control, respect for others, expressing feelings tactfully, or something similar.* Topic and length are your decision. You can review the writing with Justice, correcting for grammar and discussing content.

2. *Look up, define, and use in a sentence ten dictionary words (three syllables or more).* If a teen talks tough often, you may need a dictionary in every room. One mother's attitude was "If you talk like that, you need a bigger vocabulary." By the time her son was fourteen, he had the top vocabulary scores in his high school.

3. *Find and define ten words with a z in the middle.* Or define fifteen words ending in *ion.* To play with Oxford's head a little, try, "You can't leave the kitchen table until you find ten words that begin with *qx.*"

4. *Levy a monetary fine for nasty talk.* Teenagers may like to talk poorly, but they don't like to be poor.

The opposite of nasty talk is respect. What perks can Gabby earn by being pleasant, say, for two days? Gradually lengthen the time required to earn them. Ask Gabby what she'd like to earn, her request within reason, of course. Otherwise, it could be "an unchaperoned trip to Daytona Beach."

What constitutes nasty talk is your judgment, not Gabby's. Debate it with her, and she'll give you that look that says, "What? I didn't say anything. What tone of voice? My lips never moved."

# A Bad Age

Dear Dr. Ray,

My kids (ages eleven and fourteen) seldom get blatantly disrespectful, but they give me eye rolls; half-joking *duhs*; "Yeah, right, Mom." My friends tell me, "Just let it pass; it's the age."

*Hmmm ...*

Yes, it is the age—not the age of adolescence, as your friends think, but the age of toleration for disrespect.

Sometimes I will tease a parent: "What would your mother have done had you talked to her the way your son [or daughter] it talking to you?"

"Oh, I never would have done that to my mother."

"Why? You were thirteen years old once. If teens are so full of attitude, why weren't you?"

"Well, I may have felt like it, but I didn't do it. I just knew something would happen."

"What?"

"I don't know."

"Why didn't you know?"

"Because it never happened."

"Why not?"

"Because I never did it."

"Why didn't you do it?"

"I knew something would happen."

"What?"

"I don't know."

And on it goes, like old an Abbot and Costello routine. But it speaks generational reality. More parents then demanded respect—verbal and nonverbal—and kids knew it and acted—and looked—accordingly.

Your children's subtle disrespect—though no disrespect is subtle if you can perceive it—puts a face to a broader mentality that undercuts parents today and hurts kids. It's the "He's not really bad comparatively" mentality. Because what Conan is doing is not extreme, a parent should be more accepting of—perhaps even grateful for—minor misconduct, the normal stuff of kidhood. Because some trouble is typical, it will resolve on its own. So goes the reasoning.

The reasoning is faulty. It ignores the core question of parenthood: What kind of person do I wish to raise? Parents can more often than not raise a youngster "not on drugs" by following cultural norms. To raise a child of exceptional character, however, almost always entails living by standards well above the group's. The question is not "Is this behavior all that bad?" The question is "Is this behavior all that good?"

---

The question is not "Is this behavior all that bad?"
The question is "Is this behavior all that good?"

---

Your friends are right in one sense. As kids get older, they become ever more skilled at walking the line between open expression and disrespect. Four-year-olds have little finesse. When they're mad, the whole world knows. Fourteen-year-olds can be so smooth that only an hour later does a parent realize, "Hey, I was insulted."

To assess whether tolerating your youngsters' disparaging looks and covert commentary is wise, try this test. For the next month, whatever your kids do to you, do the same to your best friend, your boss, or your pastor. So whenever anyone says or does anything you disagree with or don't like, simply respond, "Well, duh!" or "Yeah, right" or the ubiquitous "Whatever." At the end of the month, ask, "Do you like the new me?" See if they reply, "Well, I do love the way you let me so easily know how you feel. I never have to wonder what you're thinking." Yeah, right.

When removed from the rationale "that's just what kids do," the harmless stuff doesn't seem so harmless.

I can imagine myself standing before a judge and pleading, "Come on, Your Honor, you get all kinds of big crime in here: murder, robbery, arson. I don't do any of that. It's not like I'm a felon or anything."

While eye rolling isn't on par with joint rolling, is it wrong, or isn't it? The parent who says, "No, I don't think it is," doesn't need to do anything about it. The parent who says, "Yes, it is" does.

Respect is a package. It has both overt and covert components. To reduce your teens' snotitude, go zero tolerance. Permit none of it, which means put a price tag on it. For example, one extra chore. Forty push-ups per eye roll. Look up, define, and use in a sentence ten synonyms for *whatever*. A teenage picture of you on Art's mirror for every five insolent looks.

Surly expressions can become a style, a reflex reaction. And the silent stuff lays a base for more vocal stuff. Stop it all, and you'll feel a whole lot more appreciated, and your kids will be a whole lot nicer.

Agreed? No? Oh, puh-lease, get real.

# Addenda

Dear Dr. Ray,

I have to say, "I mean it!" or "Now!" to get my kids to listen. And they're starting to ignore me even then.

*Help. I Mean It.*

You're resorting to what I call addenda. It's a habit that can trap parents.

What are addenda? They are words or sentences tacked on to a request or command, designed to add weight to the earlier words.

Here are seven top parental addenda: (1) I mean it! (2) Did you hear me? (3) Now! (4) I'm not going to say it again! (5) I said (then repeat original directive). (6) Don't make me come over there! (7) First, middle, last name (varies from child to child).

What's the downside of addenda? First, as you are finding out, they don't work. Initially, they may grab some attention or compliance, but their effect fades with time.

Second, they send a false message. Do you mean it only when you say, "I mean it"? If you don't say "I mean it," does that mean you don't mean it and you are just talking to hear yourself talk?

Do you mean it
only when you say, "I mean it"?

Third, addenda tend to get loud. The more they're used, the higher their volume. And it's a short jump from high decibels to high emotions. Then the emotions are doing more talking than the words, no matter how many.

Most important, when disciplining, the persuasive power of words isn't improved with more words. If a twelve-word request isn't heeded, why would a fifteen-word one be? Successful discipline lies in its consequences, not its words. Addenda just add weight to words that have lost their weight.

To withdraw from addenda, go cold turkey. Stop using them. Replace them with addenda that do add weight to your words.

There is one kind of addenda that works pretty well. Here are examples: "Hazel, please pick up the family room." Addendum: "If I ask you again, you'll vacuum it too." "Butkus, leave your brother alone." Addendum: "Or you'll sit with your head down at the table for ten minutes." "Don't nag me, Constance." Addendum: "The next time you ask, the answer is no."

Action addenda work; word addenda don't, not long-term anyway. Authority comes from meaning what you say. And meaning what you say comes from backing your words with action, not more words.

So don't do it anymore, okay? I mean it. I'm not writing just to see myself write. Do you read me?

# From Slander to Libel

Dear Dr. Ray,

I make my older kids write essays of apology if they are disrespectful. But sometimes the essays are as disrespectful as the original disrespect.

*Déjà Vu*

Are you thinking that what looked to be "fit the crime" discipline is backfiring? Rather than nudging Agatha and Christie to ponder the nature of their commentary, you are provoking them to more misconduct? Instead of shaping respect, are you inciting disrespect? Would it be better to skip the essay, thus removing a venue for more critique?

Parenting law #104: No matter how well-thought-out your discipline, a child can still find ways to circumvent it.

Parenting gurus typically intone: "Properly discipline Angel, and she will understand, accept, and be grateful. No arguments, no resistance, no escalation, just cooperation." I love fantasy.

When youngsters don't agree with what you're doing as a parent—surprise!—they let you know somehow. This doesn't mean the idea is weak; more often, it means the reverse. Edgar Allan wants you to abandon it because it is working.

An advantage of being the parent is that you don't have to outthink the kids. You set the conditions:

1. *Respect is expected, whether verbal or written.* Essay nastiness not only invalidates the essay but leads to a do-over, perhaps a longer one.

2. *Disrespect anywhere within the essay nullifies the whole essay, not just the libelous sections.* Otherwise, savvy kids will just expunge those sections and recycle those that bespeak what a remarkable parent you are to have raised such fine offspring.

3. *A scolding screed can carry an unwritten consequence—say,* two extra chores or weeding the front flower bed.

Much oral disrespect is impulsive or emotional. Written disrespect is more premeditated. It's a calculated critique on your parenthood. It may need a more calculated response.

---

Sometimes an essay is just a written fit.

---

Discipline teaches through repetition. Because Edgar Allan writes poorly in his first ten essays, that doesn't mean he won't become more self-controlled in essays number eleven through infinity.

Sometimes an essay is just a written fit. At least it isn't screaming. Unless it's written in CAPS.

# I Say, You Say

Dear Dr. Ray,

No matter what I say, my son always has a comeback. What do you do with kids who always have to have the last word?

*Next to Last*

It depends on what the last word is. Is it, "Gosh, Mom, you always make so much sense"? Or, "Most certainly I'll finish my homework before I rake the leaves"? How about, "Sometimes I honestly do feel like arguing with you, Mother, but I know you'll win because you're so much wiser about life than I am"?

If your son's retorts are anything like these, I would: (a) kiss him, (b) nominate him for PTA poster boy of the year, (c) show him off in public as much as possible, or (d) have him assessed psychiatrically.

I'm going to take a wild guess and assume that you haven't received anything similar. Rather, your son is arguing or challenging your rules and decisions. He flings "Your way or the highway" only when you ask or tell him something he finds disagreeable. Is that safe to say?

The frequency of your son's comebacks is directly related to the frequency of your comebacks. That is, he'll argue as long as you do. What does he have to lose? He's counting on any one of several outcomes: (1) you'll change your mind (primary goal), (2) you'll collapse from the volume of words (secondary goal), (3) you'll stand your ground but only after paying an exhausting price ("salvage something" goal).

---

The frequency of your son's comebacks
is directly related to the
frequency of your comebacks.

---

As long as you allow Sherlock to dictate the direction of the dialogue, he will. Send a signal: Arguing will gain him nothing; it will cost him.

"Sherlock, be home by 7:00 p.m." That's really all you need to say. You've told him why: for dinner, schoolwork, to visit Uncle Buck, whatever. He's lived with you for years. You've explained yourself. Seldom do you need to elaborate. Nevertheless, Sherlock rebuts, "Why do I have to come home at 7:00? I don't want to go to Aunt Clara's."

Whatever you say next to explain further is pretty much irrelevant because it will elicit the same response from Sherlock: more debate. The word spiral spins a while longer until one or both of you really gets mad, one of you gives in (guess who?), or one of you goes to Aunt Clara's but is miserable about it (guess who?).

Stopping this cycle falls on you. Why? Because you're the parent, for one, and because Sherlock likes things just as they are, for another. What are your options then?

You could pull out and pull away. You've made your point; you don't want to keep on keeping on. You could give Sherlock a look that says, "You'd better think carefully about saying any more because you've already pushed too hard."

Have you noticed that sometime between the previous generation and the present, the "look" has disappeared? Parents of the past were much more adept at sending looks that spoke volumes.

No more words, warnings, and wrangling were needed: Once you saw that look, you knew to back off because pushing more would be consequential, so to speak.

Why do kids argue so much? Because they want to and because they're allowed.

Are they truly interested in understanding our ways? If so, wouldn't you think that at least once or twice a year, after twenty-seven minutes of nonstop negotiating, Sherlock would look up enlightened and confess, "You know, Mom, I don't always agree with the way you do things, but if we bicker long enough, it does become clearer. Thanks, Mom, for taking so much time to explain."

# Express Yourself

Dear Dr. Ray,

If my son tells me one more time, "You just want things your way," I'll scream. I do want to raise him my way, not his.

*Second-Guessing My Ways*

Nonsense child-rearing notion: In the name of open communication, parents should allow children wide latitude to air their feelings. Much of what was once considered disrespect is now shielded behind emotional venting. Miranda's perspective, however meanly meant and said, must be affirmed lest she become a pent-up, stifled Stepford child. Erring on the safe side, many parents allow what their head and gut tell them is pretty insulting stuff.

> Much of what was once considered disrespect is now shielded behind emotional venting.

Kids do have a right to speak and to be heard. That right, however, ends where nastiness begins. Where, parents ask, to draw the line separating healthy openness from bad intent? A guideline: Feelings that are expressed with regard for another's feelings are acceptable; those that batter another's feelings are not.

Some standard kid gripes: "You don't like me," "I don't like you," "You like Charity better," "You're unfair," "You're mean,"

"You're old-fashioned," "You're a parent" (this is often what they're really saying). Most parents tolerate kid commentary of this ilk if it stays restrained. In other words, I don't like it, but I'll allow it if it doesn't get ugly.

Your son's repeated accusation may not be all that ugly, but it is wearing. And your son probably senses this. You'd like to stop him but wonder how much you'd be curtailing his freedom of speech.

Your son's First Amendment rights, like those of grown-ups', aren't limitless. He has moved beyond an occasional burst of opinion to a steady insult.

"You just like things your way" does ring of truth, though. You do know better how to raise him than he does.

A principle of propaganda: "Repeat a lie often enough, and people will come to believe it." Rather than speaking truth, your son is repeating a lie. He is reinforcing in his own mind nonsense.

Trust your instincts. If you don't like this running accusation, if you think it's ridiculous, stop it. You're stifling nothing more than a falsehood. Have your way on this.

# Words without End

Dear Dr. Ray,

How can I keep my kids from nagging? They hammer away at me until I either cave in or lose my temper. And the more frustrated I get, the harder they push.

*Nagging Fears*

Nagging illustrates a great paradox of parenthood. The more parents nag, the less kids respond. The more kids nag, the more parents respond. Are they smarter than we are? No, but they have more stamina.

If nagging didn't succeed even occasionally, kids wouldn't do it. Kids deduce this after a few years of life. Parents deduce it after a few kids.

Effective nagging is simple: Use words to achieve a goal. The short-term goal is to get what you want. The long-term goal is to soften a parent's resistance to future nagging.

Relative to parents, children are powerless. They don't have control over their surroundings, as we do. So with words—thousands—comes their persuasive power. Kids count on our ears' tiring long before their vocal cords do.

There are two times when kids are more persistent than normal. (Normal persistence is considered five to ten nags per hour.) The first is when they really want something. The second is the more urgent "really, really want something."

You are weighing whether to grant Desiree a special treat or privilege. She can't chance that you'll decide based solely upon the merits, so she dramatically kicks up her level of pleading, begging, and whining. One nagging reacting response is "You're not letting me think about this, and that's not in your interests."

If you can reach deep within and tap a reservoir of resolve, ignore all nagging words. That's easy for me to write. I'm listening to music. I can hit Pause if I want. Kids don't have Pause options. After you've said no six times to "Mom, can I ride the triple-spiral demon a seventh time?" act as though no words are coming from Constance. In time—anywhere between a minute and a decade—she should wind down.

> Nagging illustrates a great paradox
> of parenthood. The more parents nag,
> the less kids respond. The more kids
> nag, the more parents respond.

If you're like me and doubt your ability to stay oblivious for thousands of words at a time, or if you simply don't want to endure it, you could implement a gag order: "Tucker, if you nag, you will nag to your mirror in your room" or "You will write fifty times, 'Nagging is not a good way to communicate.'" Would fifty times constitute written nagging?

One mother simply asked, "Are you nagging?" She really was saying, "Don't nag, or you won't like my answer." The kids knew the answer. They'd heard it a few dozen times before "Are you nagging?" alone silenced them.

Once kids realize that you will not be nagged to fatigue, they will have to find other ways to get what they want. That's good, I think.

So try these ideas. Okay? Just for a few weeks. See if they work. All right? Just a couple of them. Promise? You asked the question, so you can at least consider the answer. C'mon. What've you got to lose? Are you even listening to me?

# Wait Until Someone Gets Home

Dear Dr. Ray,

I'm a grandmother. Many in my generation heard, "Wait until your father gets home," if we misbehaved. Kids these days don't hear this very often. Good or bad, in your opinion?

*Waiting*

It depends. (Don't shrink-type answers sometimes drive you crazy?)

Why don't kids hear this once stock child-rearing caution all that much anymore?

One, the dad-at-work, mom-at-home family profile is no longer the norm. Only a minority of families now fit it. Therefore, logistics permit fewer kids to be so warned. One would think that with so many dual-employed parents, some frustrated fathers might also warn, "Wait until your mother gets home."

Two, even some stay-at-home moms never utter, "Wait until your father gets home." That's because the authority is already home: Mom. More mothers lament that they set the rules and discipline, while Dad is "Mr. Nice Guy" or "Disney Dad" or "Mr. Laid-Back." When Mom does most of the disciplining, she doesn't wait for backup.

Three, experts — I get nervous using that word — stress that moms need authority equal to dads. Relying on an unseen enforcer to give Mom some discipline oomph puts Dad in an unfair spot while lowering Mom's authority in kids' eyes.

Day to day, a mother with authority benefits all members of the family. For herself, she gains respect and cooperation. Little kids particularly act better when discipline is immediate rather than delayed.

To the kids she gives predictability and security. She is ready to act to keep the household running smoothly. It will not be turmoil for nine hours until the hammer comes down.

To her husband she gives respite. He doesn't enter warily, anticipating a litany of upheaval to fix, along with a frazzled spouse. Mom may be weary from the day's demands, but discipline frustration won't be most of it.

What, then, is the "depends" part of my answer to your question? In smooth-running families, the dual authority of Mom and Dad is one. So if Bliss pushes on Mom all day, even though Mom handled it, Dad lends his support. His rationale? Bliss gave his wife recurrent grief, and he will act to teach a more memorable lesson.

> In smooth-running families, the dual authority of Mom and Dad is one.

When our children were younger, I could sense when my wife was having a rough day. She'd meet me in the garage, holding two children by their arms, mumbling in Seussian rhyme, "I do not want them in my hair; I do not want them here or there. You'd better take them, Ray I am. For I am angry, yes, I am."

From years of communication training, I recognized these early signs of overload. I knew to add my authority to my wife's. The children learned that their mother and I were a team. You rattle her; you rattle me.

Therefore, their mom seldom had to say, "Wait until your father comes home." They knew that if Mom was rhyming when Father came home, they were in bigger trouble. Yes, indeed, they'd better heed.

# 5

# Trouble Trademarks of the Teens

Every stage of childhood presents its own trademark misbehaviors. Preschoolers display temper tempests, bedtime bad times, meal ordeals, toy litter, disrespect. Elementary-age kids lean toward to sibling quibbling, tattling, homework hassles, disrespect. From the teens come chore shirking, disrespect, curfew contention, disrespect, schoolwork avoidance, disrespect …

Toning down disrespect has its own section in this book; it deserves it. Here we'll tackle a few other trouble trademarks of the teen years.

# Kids Don't Make Good Parents

Dear Dr. Ray,

My fourteen- and twelve-year-old sons bicker constantly, sometimes leading to all-out battles. I've read that I should let them resolve their own conflicts, but I'm afraid they'll hurt each other long before they learn to get along.

*On the Sidelines*

Would you allow your fourteen-year-old to set his brother's bedtime? How about his school schedule? Would you let him decide what constitutes back talk and then discipline? Of course not. Why? Because he's not his brother's mother. And he has neither the maturity nor the judgment to raise his brother well.

Letting siblings resolve their conflicts while parents stand down is standard expert advice. The hope is that kids will figure out through constant jockeying, sparring, and free-for-alling how to get along. As long as parents don't "intrude," children will regulate themselves and therefore more readily accept their self-guidance.

Like most psychologically correct child-rearing notions, this one sounds good on paper. It sure would be nice if kids could do some of this parenting stuff themselves. And they could, *if* they are close in age and size, and *if* they truly want to get along, and *if* they don't hurt each other first, and *if* your house can survive their assault, and *if* you can weather the chaos—then maybe Rocky and Bruno can negotiate their way to an uneasy truce.

In the real world of parenthood, paper ideas can get shredded by real kids. First, likely your fourteen-year-old is bigger, stronger, smarter, and overall just a tougher opponent than his younger brother. Why would he feel compelled to work something out that surrenders his status? The drive to win begins young. It's not likely that a dominant sibling will give away his advantage.

Then too, do you want to remain passive while the boys torment, name-call, hit, and overall mistreat each other in the name of conflict resolution? Not only will the "weaker" child routinely end up losing, but a whole lot of mutual meanness will be unleashed by both. Kids are wonderfully resilient, but a relentless exchange of words or fists can take its toll on the strongest of sibling bonds.

Third, a parent's duty is to protect. When we allow brothers and sisters to blast their way to a solution—notice I didn't say "resolution"—we abdicate the responsibility to shield them from hurt, especially hurt caused by family members. Open-ended permission to settle differences can be license for filial warfare.

---

Open-ended permission to settle differences can be license for filial warfare.

---

You set the conditions. Conflict resolution can be practiced only within the context of your parameters: no hitting, no name-calling, no head butting, no gouging, no soap in the eyes, no jumping off the ropes (big-time wrestling rules). Kids are quicker to work out their disagreements when they know the rules of the game. Of course, if they break the rules, you are there to enforce justice.

It's confusing and exhausting to jump in at every squeak and squabble. For the little stuff, sometimes cooperation will follow a "work it out peacefully, or you both will [enter shared discipline here]." After all, enemies will ally themselves when facing a common adversary.

# Testing the Sibling Bond

Dear Dr. Ray,

Any words for dealing with a fifteen-year-old who demeans his two younger sisters (ages thirteen and nine)—sometimes abusively so?

*Hurting with Them*

Yes. Stop him.

The sibling bond can be bent, twisted, hammered, and still hold. But why allow it to be so tested? Because a relationship can survive a battering doesn't mean the battering is good for it. I might stagger up after a face-first fall down a flight of stairs, but the fall isn't beneficial for me.

Parents will permit some sibling-on-sibling maltreatment because others—experts, family, friends—opine that siblings naturally argue, clash, and assault one another. Some expert types go further and declare that it is developmentally sound for sibs to tangle, as that perfects conflict-resolution skills. I wonder if such experts were only children.

Others say, "Don't worry. While the sibling bond can take a real licking, in the end it'll keep on ticking." I say, "Such a licking usually only leads to a ticking off—of all parties."

A big brother or sister enjoys elevated stature in a littler one's eyes. He or she is seen as grown-up or a role model, even a protector. The relationship, however, can be fractured when an older sibling disdains the family's "lesser beings."

The ill effects can be heard in remarks like "He's such a jerk," "Make him leave me alone," "I really like it when he's not home," "Does he have to come along?" Sure, some of this is said by most siblings at one time or another. But it's the number and tension that reveal the degree of resentment.

Worse, the tormenting can be pointed laser-like at a highly sensitive spot: appearance, intellect, grades, weight, taking a toll on the younger's ego, confidence, or emotions. Your girls want your protection, as they are ill-equipped to self-protect.

Consider, too, your son's well-being. By being allowed to hurt, he loses a warm relationship with siblings. He also learns to say whatever whenever. That's not a habit anyone—not just a littler sister—likes.

To repeat my first words: stop him. Words alone, though, won't do that. Action, firm and certain, is needed. Levy a consequence commensurate with his behavior. If you believe he is major nasty to his sisters—and you seem to believe so—let your discipline reflects this. Examples: a full-day loss of all privileges; a five-hundred-word written apology, including why he's grateful to have sisters; assuming all of a sister's chores for three days; writing twenty-five good things about his sister. If he says, "There aren't twenty-five good things about her," you could answer what one feisty mom did: "Make them up; I do with your father."

Is your aim to stop all mistreatment or just to tone it down to "normal"? "Normal" still implies some amount of mistreatment. Is this what you wish to allow?

> The sibling bond can be bent,
> twisted, hammered, and still hold.
> But why allow it to be so tested?

Your son's attitude toward his sisters probably won't improve overnight. But his conduct should improve quickly, as he feels the cost of showing disdain.

When a child isn't permitted to be nasty to a sibling, he has two options: either ignore her or act nicer. Fortunately, most kids act nicer. They have to. They live in the same house.

# To Fee or Not to Fee

Dear Dr. Ray,

My husband and I disagree about giving allowances to our two sons, ages twelve and fourteen. He says they live here, so they should not be paid for helping. I think allowances have benefits.

*Fee or Free*

As a psychologist and therefore inclined to find a settlement, my slant on allowances is somewhere between yours and your husband's.

Because kids are part of the family—though the older ones may be embarrassed about it, especially in public—it makes sense to have some fee-free family duties. The house is everybody's, so its care is everybody's.

Family duties might include making beds, hauling out trash, setting the table, keeping their rooms fumigated—certainly not too much to ask for the multiple benefits they receive free from you. Family duties teach that all work does not deserve recompense. Such is good preparation for spousehood.

Other duties—washing dishes, cleaning house, weeding—might be "wage chores" earning allowance money. Wage chores give kids the chance to learn to earn. Such is good preparation for adulthood.

Family chores precede wage chores. All family work must be completed before the privilege of earning an allowance begins. Otherwise, the kids will grab for the money chores first, leaving the family duties to Mom and Pop, who are supposed to work around the house for free.

> All family work must be
> completed before the privilege
> of earning an allowance begins.

What's a good allowance number? Your call. A guideline: Reflect the real world. Giving Forbes five dollars a week for feeding two goldfish and taking his clothes to the washer every Tuesday is a very generous wage. Actually, it's excessive. Translated into an hourly rate, it comes to $712. Even professional goldfish keepers don't earn that; only psychologists do. Then again, awarding one dollar a week for converting the garage to a family room and reseeding the lawn is serf labor. You know what's fair, what you can afford, and Forbes's reliability rate.

Allowances are a multibenefit package. One, they teach kids to delay gratification. Bedford straightens his bunk Monday through Friday and has to wait for his salary until Saturday. Not too often in the adult work world does one get paid the instant he finishes a task.

Two, allowances reduce financial friction. Parents who give little or no allowance, instead judging money requests individually, could run into cash clashes, as the kids think their needs (a designer ball bat or a twenty-seven-speed hair dryer) are more critical to their well-being than parents do.

Three, allowances are sound financial leverage. Bedford's bunk isn't made, so part of his allowance can go from his pocket into yours. You did his work, and belonging to Local 172 of the Bed Makers Motherhood Union, you can charge prevailing wage.

Last, allowances teach priorities. Chase will find firsthand that money supply is limited, something he won't realize when First Community Mom and Dad are the bank. Thus, he's forced to choose which extravagance he can afford, the remote-controlled ball glove or the commando rocks.

One mom of teens fined her kids for spewing any nasty words. She had a list of twenty-five-cent, fifty-cent, and dollar words. If her kids were going to use cheap language, it was going to cost them.

# A Parent's Prerogative

Dear Dr. Ray,

My fourteen-year-old son's friends receive more allowance for far less work than he does. It's an ongoing argument between us. Do I need to reassess?

*Stingy?*

Of three possible answers—yes, I don't know, and no—I'll choose the latter two.

I don't know. Perhaps you are giving your son a buck a month for cleaning the basement, each sibling's room, and both cars. If so, perhaps he does have a case. On the other hand, if the difference between your son's money-to-work ratio and his friends' reflects their doing little to be reimbursed a lot, then he has no claim. This latter scenario is the much more common.

Teens regularly base their position upon one question: How can all those parents be wrong and you be right? Quick answer: They are, and I am. Kids promote parenting by consensus—if the consensus is in their favor, that is. Your son would never bring to your attention any child in the western hemisphere who works harder for less than he does. No, that parent is even more Neanderthal than you are. And he certainly would never point out where and how he has it better than most. That would mean you are right and all those other parents are wrong. Uh huh.

In matters of morals and responsibility, the majority doesn't always provide imitation-worthy standards. Doubting yourself because others have lower standards—more reasonable, according to your son—is not a good reason to lower your standards.

Too, should you be on the stingy end of the work-for-allowance continuum, so? If you polled a hundred parents and only eleven agreed with you, so? (Am I sounding like a snotty sibling yet?) You are his parent; they are not. This reality affords you great latitude in making those decisions you believe are best for your child. More reality: Your way is often the right way because you *are* the parent. You have the right to determine what is right for you and your family.

> Your way is often the right way
> because you *are* the parent.

If you give no allowance, I may not agree with you, nor perhaps would most other parents. Again, so? The question is not "Are you being a 'proper' parent?" The question is "Do you have the parental right to decide?" If not you, who?

To be sure, a parent can make bad decisions. She can cling to attitudes and practices that only make things worse. That said, different is not necessarily wrong. Often it's better.

But you don't need me to agree with you on that.

# Many Teens Make Light Work

Dear Dr. Ray,

Two teenagers, able-bodied, chore-resistant.

*Working Alone*

One psychologist, able-minded, chore-endorsing.

I asked a group of about fifty parents, "How many of you are getting the help you'd like around the house from your teens?" Three parents raised their hands. The others promptly tagged them show-offs or liars.

I asked further, "If not, why not?" Answers: (1) The kids' lives are so busy; not much time is left for chores. (2) We don't ask all that much. (3) The kids have outside jobs. (4) Reason number one: It's too much of a hassle to get cooperation. It's easier just to do it ourselves.

Small-business owners know that a major obstacle to growth is finding reliable help, particularly young people with a solid work ethic. Such qualities don't develop naturally with age. They need consistent parental push. So how do you push without getting tired yourself?

Since I, too, have a small business — a family of twelve — I'll push ahead.

*Set the schedule.* How many rooms are in your house? How many kids? Divide the number of rooms by the number of kids (my wife counted me as one child, sometimes two). The answer is the number of rooms each person "owns." List on paper — placed inside a cabinet, on a door, near the toilet, whatever—all that's needed to maintain that room. Though you might choose a room or two for yourself, you are a supervisor, part of upper-level management.

How to ensure the rooms are cared for in a timely manner?

"Mom, can Heloise come over?" "Sure, if your rooms are done."

"Mom, will you iron my shirt?" "Okay, did you take out the trash for me yet?"

Privileges don't begin until responsibilities end. The goodies of teen life are not entitlements of age. They are privileges of the working class.

> The goodies of teen life are not entitlements of age. They are privileges of the working class.

*Jar the jobs.* On small pieces of paper, write all your household jobs: vacuum dining room, clean toilets, sweep garage floor, clean out refrigerator, arrange closet, paint car, rotate its tires. For a range of misbehavior, the job jar is the consequence. "Please reach in—blindly—and grab a job." If your kids are going to act bad, at least your home will look good.

*Answer questions with questions*—a standard psychology trick.

"Mom, can I use the computer?" "Sure, is the family room picked up?"

"Will you take me to practice?" "I'd like to; will the dishes be done first?" (By the child, that is.)

"Can Eve stay overnight Friday after skating?" "Can you clean the house? I wouldn't want Eve to have to sleep in a messy place."

# Standing Strong

The typical teen makes daily requests of parents. Link those requests—whenever and however you see fit—to willing helpfulness.

Farmers of 150 years ago had it right: big kids = big bodies = big help. An advantage of having teens is having domestic help. As your kids grow, your days of hard, lonely labor should shrink.

# A Kid's Room: No Place for a House

Dear Dr. Ray,

Any suggestions for getting kids to keep their rooms halfway livable? My children are eleven and fourteen, and their standard comeback is, "It's my room. Why can't I keep it the way I want?"

*It's My House*

"I'm afraid to go in there without a wilderness survival kit and an oxygen mask." "Two of her sisters accidentally stumbled into her bedroom about a year ago and were gone for days." "We call his room 'Star Trek': to venture in is to 'boldly go where no mom has gone before.'"

> We call his room "Star Trek":
> to venture in is to "boldly go
> where no mom has gone before."

As colorfully as parents can image a messy room, so, too, can they sanitize it. One mother, in a fit of frustration, collected all the debris decomposing on her son's floor and piled it on his bed; the mound brushed the ceiling. Undaunted, her son slept on his newly found floor the next three nights. He finally did relent and began to sort through the stack. Maybe he needed his sweatpants, buried somewhere near the bottom.

During a cleansing frenzy, another parent threw every bit of stuff clogging up his son's bedroom out the window. Returning from school, Taylor saw the shrubs wearing his gym shorts and T-shirts. To paraphrase the saying, one picture is worth a thousand naggings. Things were borderline straightened after that.

Dramatics like these can send a message, but they tend to be short-lived. A few days later, Comfort's room returns to its pre-habitable state. Besides, the cleansing is parent-performed, not child-performed. More durable solutions to ruined rooms begin with:

How do you want to view your kids' rooms? (From three miles away?) Parental perspective here is divided. For some, a youngster's room is his retreat: as long as the door is sealed—steel-encased door with a twelve-inch external deadbolt—all within is out of sight and out of mind. Others reason, "It's Dusty's room, but it's my house, and I don't want any of my house below city health code."

Your stance determines your approach. The "closed door" requires less effort. The room just exists, and the hope is that Sandy will eventually develop some motivation to keep his turf navigable. Sometimes this happens; other times it doesn't, not until a youngster has his own place. Maybe.

To speed up the transformation, do not invade Sandy's room to pick up clothes, bed sheets, or miscellaneous materials that need laundering, tailoring, or general parental service. He can: (1) bring the clothes to the laundry room himself, (2) wash all washables himself, (3) repair and mend his own possessions.

The "It's his room, but it's my house" philosophy takes more energy, but it usually results in a better-kept room.

Step 1: Set up room inspection time; for example, Wednesday at 6:30 p.m. and Saturday at 11:00 a.m. If conditions initially are overwhelming, you might need daily—hourly?—visits. Hazmat gear can be ordered online.

Step 2. What is the cost for a messy room? *Messy* is one of those squishy terms that kids like to personally define, so maybe you'd better define *messy* or its partners — *unlivable* and *trashed*. What are some costs? Suggestions upcoming in the "filthy room" question.

There's an upside to a messy room. If you run out of storage space in the garage or shed, you can always park the lawn tractor in Forrest's room. He will never know it's there.

# Good by Comparison

Dear Dr. Ray,

I have long been upset over the condition of my fourteen-year-old's room. When my friend saw it, she laughed and told me I'm overreacting; I should see her son's room.

*Calm Down and Lighten Up?*

Why should you see her son's room? In your eyes, your son's room is plenty gross enough. Before I answer you, let's answer your friend on several levels.

Level 1: She says her son's room is less habitable than your son's. All that really tells you is that there are two rooms in your homes in a trashed state. While her son's may be worse, she is less displeased by it. That's her prerogative, but it is irrelevant to you. Your room standards are unique to you.

Level 2: Should you take solace that there are kids sloppier than yours? Any parent can find children less cooperative than their own. There is little comfort in comparing favorably to others if their standards are lower. That's easy to do. The question is, how do you compare to your own standards?

Level 3: Your friend is implying that your son is age-typical, at least where tidiness is the measure. True. Most teenage boys have rooms that make landfills look like flower gardens. On one hand, that can be reassuring. It can keep you from reading too much into your son's room state. It is not atypical, bizarre, or pathological. That itself can temper overreacting, as your friend says.

On the other hand, just because your son's room meets peer code, that doesn't mean it meets Mom code. What is tidy to a boy may not be so to his mother, who just happens to own the house that surrounds the room. You set the conditions that will teach your son to cooperate with legitimate rules even when he does not agree with them. And that's a virtue that's fast being ignored in our culture.

Level 4: You need to chill because your son's not doing anything all that bad; so says your friend. Granted, disheveled rooms are low on most parents' priority lists. But low doesn't mean ignore.

If your friend thinks you're overreacting, and you admit to some, you can always tone down the nagging or harangues. But you don't have to tone down your expectations. It's one thing to rethink your discipline style. It's quite another to abandon your discipline altogether.

Level 5: You should measure your parenting by the group. If the majority's standards are slipping, it's unwise to use the majority as a measure. If all the other parents jump into the lake, are you going to jump in too? Or, closer to home, if all the other parents live beside a trashed room, are you going to live beside one too?

> If the majority's standards are slipping,
> it's unwise to use the majority as a measure.

Now, on to cleaning that room somewhat:
1. Send Dusty there periodically—tie a rope around his waist so you can pull him out if trapped—and he can't come out until it's straightened.
2. You sanitize it but charge him. You're union, aren't you?

3. With a large trash bag, sort through the debris. Naturally, you can't know always what he does or doesn't value.
4. Room inspection is 6:00 p.m. Wednesday and 11:00 a.m. Saturday. Not tidied sufficiently earns an hour of extra chores, plus the cleaned room, before privileges begin.

Lest you're thinking, "How did Dr. Ray get all those levels of interpretation from just a couple of statements?" well, I'm a shrink. I'm practiced at overanalyzing. And I'm a parent. I'm practiced at overreacting.

# Afraid of Commitment

Dear Dr. Ray,

How hard and long should a parent push a child to stay committed to an activity for which he has lost his initial enthusiasm?

*Committed for Now*

When I was twelve years old, my parents purchased an organ for my younger sister. "Me, too," I said. "I want to learn." Several lessons later, just about the time my zeal for music was going flat, my teacher told my father, "He has a gift." The woman talked too much.

That convinced Pop. The man listened too much. His son would learn to play the organ. The months dragged on, and I was sure both my instructor and my father were singing the wrong tune. Regularly I argued, "It's not like I'm going to be a professional or something." Ah, the cocksure prophecy of youth.

Once past my initial resistance and gaining skill despite my worst efforts, this organ idea sounded better. Some years later, I turned professional (or something), entertaining in restaurants for nearly a decade, earning enough money to graduate college debt-free along with having learned a skill for a lifetime. Had my father yielded to my shortsightedness, I would have quit in the first few months, never knowing what I had denied myself.

How long to insist that a youngster remain committed depends upon many factors.

- *Talent.* How naturally is he gifted? It would seem that the more skilled, the longer he should allow for the rewards to show.
- *Competition.* Is Nielsen's interest flagging because of other more beckoning pursuits — television, computer games, phone? Kids' options for entertainment are surging. It is all too easy for the shallow to crowd out the worthwhile. Limiting the time stealers allows more that's time-profitable.
- *Investment.* How long did Orville plead and push to take up hang gliding? Was there a startup cost? Who paid? Who pays if the activity is abandoned? Who else will be affected? Lefty may bother no one if he quits origami class, but it drags down a whole team to lose a pitcher midseason.
- *Pattern.* Is this one-time or a style? Does Constance lose interest in most everything she starts? If so, she may need to develop a little stick-to-itiveness. If it's limited to this new activity, well, maybe cliff diving is not her sport.

One mother's rule of thumb: "If you start, you're in for one season or one year, whichever comes first. No escape clause."

What if the activity requires regular practice, and follow-through is taking more commitment from the parent than the child? Give Cliburn a choice: One hour of chores can substitute for one half hour of practice. The only way to skip practice is to do double-time chores. That should reveal his level of resistance.

We all try things that over time we find we don't like. The balance lies in spending enough time and effort to find out that a particular pursuit is not for us, not so little that we prematurely conclude we're not for it.

# Underachievement: School Problem Number 1

Dear Dr. Ray,

My son is a sophomore. All his teachers say he is academically quite capable, but his grades are very poor. He seems to lack initiative.

*Tired of Pushing*

Yours is by far the most frequent school-related question parents ask me. Underachievement—a child's not working up to potential—dwarfs the incidence of other, more high-profile problems, such as school phobia and classroom disruption.

Before motivating the undermotivated, one caution: Some children who look like underachievers really aren't. Intellectual or learning struggles underlie their school struggles. Likewise, life upheaval can disrupt schoolwork. Consultation with teachers or psychologists can help rule out these connections.

That said, most kids who perform poorly in school are not hindered by learning or social or emotional struggles. They are quite able to achieve, often at a skilled level. This sounds like your son.

Typically, underachievement has been building. Aversion to schoolwork began in the earlier grades and has waxed and waned ever since. Assignments are not completed during class time. Homework sits at school or is lost, left in the bushes, "forgotten," eaten by the dog, or faked. "Honest, Mom, this is the third teacher I've had since second grade who doesn't believe in homework or tests!"

The underachieving youngster spends more of his scholastic energy skirting schoolwork than doing schoolwork. And if an internal fire flares—for whatever reason—it is short-lived.

The underachieving child is not easily moved by encouragement, rewards, and punishment. Discipline is only erratically effective because little is powerful enough to consistently overcome his apathy toward schoolwork. In short, the underachiever is the one about whom many parents lament, "We've tried everything; nothing works."

> The underachiever is the one about whom many parents lament, "We've tried everything; nothing works."

What drives certain kids to be so undriven? Some downright dislike schoolwork. To them it is boring, demanding, or meaningless. They see little purpose in it and prefer occupying their school hours with more immediate pursuits—counting passing cars, doodling, or daydreaming.

Some do have slight delays in maturity or concentration, though nothing significant enough to warrant special services. Still, they are capable of succeeding at grade level. Because it doesn't come so easily, however, they retreat or cease trying.

As immovable as underachievement can seem, it can be reversed. The "note home" is a highly structured daily plan that, if closely monitored, is unbeatable. Even Newton, as brainy as he is, won't be able to find loopholes in it.

Step 1. *Obtain a small spiral notepad.* It will be your youngster's everyday school companion. While any kind of record sheet will do, the notepad's advantage is that it's pocket-size, is hard to lose, and can provide look-backs to measure progress or see patterns.

Step 2. *Keep a daily record.* At the end of each school day or each period, Oxford is to write all assignments, incomplete classwork, failed tests, and anything else you think relevant.

Step 3. *Ensure accuracy.* Oxford is to ask his teacher(s) to initial the pad after class or school day. Teachers initial only if everything is listed correctly. Otherwise, they offer neither corrections nor initials. If Oxford has finished all work in all classes, he writes "all work is done" and seeks the confirming initials.

Step 4. *Schoolwork is completed immediately after school.* Only when schoolwork is completed correctly can privileges and activities begin. Schoolwork is a priority activity.

Should Webster get a break after school to unwind? It would seem he got a break at school. He didn't do a whole lot for six hours.

Step 5. *The notepad equals privileges.* It is the ticket to television, phone, games, outdoors—everything but breathing, eating, reading, and bathroom.

What if no notepad comes home or the initials or needed books are missing? Here is the weak link, and kids know it. They are high achievers at conjuring up hard-to-confirm explanations. "We had a substitute today, and he said he won't sign anything without his lawyer reading it first." "That kid Butkus stole my book just to get me in trouble."

Whatever the reason, that notepad must arrive home, signed and ready for action. Try to validate every excuse you hear, and you're forcing yourself into a guessing game where facts are elusive.

A less structured approach is "grades by the week." Every Friday, Stanford reports his grades in each subject—initialed, of course, by his teachers. Nothing below a C—or, if his ability is well above average, a B—is acceptable. Otherwise, he will experience a significant reduction (your judgment) in perks and social movement until next Friday's report, which is, more often than not, improved. Give it some weeks to set the trend.

A third plan: Beg, borrow, or buy a copy of each of your son's books. Keep them at home. Or, get ones at his grade level from a bookstore. If anything is in question, give assignments from your books, making them longer than any from school. He'll come to see it is definitely to his benefit to bring home all books and work.

Step 6. *Persevere.* For the first twenty-two days, Patience might play with her pencil and stare off until 7:00 p.m. Underachievement is a habit, and habits take time to conquer and reverse.

Guidelines for all plans:

1. *Your position is nonnegotiable.* School is the work of children; it reaches far into their future. You are making a definite statement: At age fourteen, you do not have the choice to do or not do your schoolwork.

2. *These approaches do not initially internally motivate Stanford;* they are pure external motivation. In time, more inner internal drive will come with success. Until then, you are keeping Stanford on track with the skills ready when he does decide to push himself.

3. *Don't frustrate yourself over Stanford's pace.* Help when you think best, but otherwise let your methods do your talking. If Stanford makes his time taxing for a while, that is his choice. He is not dumb. He will move on when he tires of his self-imposed schedule.

4. *Set positive goals.* If Stanford completes all classwork at school for three days in a row, he can earn some extra

privilege. Gradually lengthen the days needed for the privilege.

These procedures almost always succeed if you stay with them. Once your son is convinced they're here to stay, he will work to make them go away. In so doing, he will no longer underachieve.

# Double Jeopardy

Dear Dr. Ray,

I've always told my children, "If you get in trouble at school, you'll be in more trouble at home." The school tells me that I should let them handle any problems there, rather than disciplining my kids a second time for the same infraction.

*Once Is Enough?*

There's a legal concept called double jeopardy. It asserts you can't try someone a second time if he's been acquitted of a crime the first time. It makes for good law but not necessarily good parenting.

Sometimes more than one response might be fitting for one "crime." Further, what another may consider a miniscule misdemeanor you may not.

In preschool, my son Andrew threw some cornmeal at another boy. The teacher saw it as nothing malicious, removed him from "cornmeal box," and told us about it.

Figuring that Andrew not only misbehaved but also cost me some business—I mean, who would want to visit a psychologist whose own kid acts up?—I asked him to explain.

"Well, Dad, I know some things are good to do, and some things are bad to do, but how can I know which is which until I try them all?" It was going to be one long year.

A fast-on-his-feet answer, I thought. Nevertheless, I told him he'd be disciplined at home for his behavior at school. My wife and I agreed: ten minutes in the corner, no Mr. Rogers (it was the one where they showed how they put makeup on the Incredible Hulk, too!), no dessert, and an early bedtime. He was our first child. By the time our tenth made the scene, I probably would have asked, "How hard did you throw it? Underhand or overhand?"

Did we overdo it? Some might think so, including Andrew's teacher. But our rationale was this: Andrew broke his teacher's rule "No throwing cornmeal." And he broke our rule "Respect your teacher's rules"—the higher rule.

> Andrew broke his teacher's rule "No throwing cornmeal." And he broke our rule "Respect your teacher's rules"—the higher rule.

Andrew's teacher's response—separation from the scene of the cornmeal melee—was a beginning. The ending was ours. We meant to send Andrew a further message. In essence, our consequences had more meat than hers.

If you believe—as we did—that your children respect their teachers' and schools' rules, you are not practicing double jeopardy by holding your children answerable to you, even if the school has addressed the trouble in its way. Others can't put limits on your discipline, which is guided by your values and morals. As a parent, you have a wide latitude in dealing with your youngster's misbehavior away from home.

Did Andrew ever throw cornmeal again? Not that we knew, but we did have to help him overcome his grain phobia.

# Admit Your Limits

Dear Dr. Ray,

I recently discovered cigarettes in my fourteen-year-old son's coat pocket. He knows how strongly I feel about this, but I'm not sure how to stop him.

*Now What?*

There's a saying that summarizes raising kids: From birth to six, you teach them; from six to twelve, you guide them; from twelve to eighteen, you pray for them. Of course, all teaching doesn't stop at age six; neither does guidance at age twelve. But most parents' praying rises dramatically with the onslaught of adolescence.

Your son's smoking brings home one of the more unsettling truths of parenthood: As kids get older, a parent's ability to directly supervise them lessens. Ultimately that's good. That's the natural course—to guide them toward their own independence and ours too. It's poor timing, though, that our influence declines faster than we're ready for. Then again, are we ever totally ready, no matter how old we or they get?

The reality: You can't stop your son from smoking—not totally anyway, for you simply can't shadow him every second of every day.

Nevertheless, once you accept your decreasing influence, you may actually increase it. How's that again?

Your son is acutely aware that you can't monitor his every move. Kids realize this before we parents do. So you're not giving away any secrets by informing him that you know he is smoking.

Most likely you've broached this subject many times. Of course, I'm assuming you don't smoke. It's a bit hard to maintain credibility while you're lighting up one after another because you're so upset over his smoking.

Tell him that you realize he can find plenty of places to secretly smoke, but you won't frazzle yourself trying to catch him. That would be a drag.

"Admit your limits" is tailored for teens because it takes some of the appeal out of sneaking behind the folks' back. The forbidden fruit is not nearly so tasty when they know you know they're tasting it.

---

> The forbidden fruit is not nearly so tasty when they know you know they're tasting it.

---

Stand firm on what you can control. There will be absolutely no smoking around you. If any cigarette paraphernalia are found, they will be thrown out, and consequence will follow. Carlton might lose his allowance for a good while, since he's burning part of his money on cigarettes anyway. Or a fine of ten dollars can be levied, to be donated to the American Cancer Society. If his clothes smell of smoke, he washes them.

Further, should you find out that your son has been smoking—from the school, his younger sister, his breath (he probably spends as much money on gum as on cigarettes)—consequences will be quick and sure.

Your message is "I can't stop you. But you know how strongly I feel. Know you'll be held accountable when this behavior comes to my attention."

The nature of teens is to behave sometimes in foolishly short-sighted ways. It's one way they learn. It's a hard way, but they force themselves into it. In time, your son is likely to quit on his own. In the meantime, you're adding motivation to quit.

6

# Give Me Liberty, or Give Me New Parents

Teens want social freedom. They want lots more than is good for them. Parents must limit that freedom—regularly. And that's when the heavy negotiations begin.

You know better than they what is best for adolescents. They don't think you do. You try to convince them you do. They don't agree. You convince longer. They get mad. Then you get mad. As the cycle spins, it's tempting to compromise because other parents give more freedom, or because the kids are relentless, or simply for peace.

To repeat: You know what's best. If your instincts say, "Go slow"—much more slowly than those around you—you'll be glad you did. So will your kids—eventually.

# The Five Ws

Dear Dr. Ray,

Ideas for better supervising teens' increasing social freedom?

*Wary and Watchful*

Interview all their friends' parents. Determine which have the highest parental supervision and vigilance. Then raise their standard for yourself and your kids.

A paramount rule for supervision of teens (or any age): Don't use a peer group of parents as your measure. Most give too much freedom too early, too loosely, and too obliviously. Supervision is 20/80 hindsight. It needs to be 20/20 hindsight and 20/10 foresight.

A wise mother—wisdom often comes through an accumulation of dumb decisions—said that to go anywhere, her kids had to answer five Ws: who, what, where, when, and why.

> Wisdom often comes through an
> accumulation of dumb decisions

*Whom* will you be with? You don't need to be a shrink to know that whom kids choose for company highly affects what they'll do when, where, and how much. Can you pick their friends? No, but you'd best pick the circle from whom they can pick. Know well—very well—their friends and, where able, their friends' parents.

*What* will you be doing? This covers not only what is planned or what is planned the first hour. Kids are notorious for starting at point A, then, once out of sight, spontaneously adding points B, C, and X to their itinerary. Changing plans is like planes changing routes. It needs to be cleared first with the control tower.

Inform Faith that you are an impulse caller. Anytime, anyplace, you could contact her just to say hi. Flouting teen protocol further, you could ask to speak to a "who"—adult or parent. Where your child's well-being is involved, embarrassment is not a mitigating factor.

*Where* are you going? Some *wheres* are flat-out off-limits, even if the *who* is Biff, the school's PTA child of the year. If you aren't familiar with the where—often another teen's house—get familiar, fast and detailed.

A five-minute call to a host parent in order to establish a safe zone is unreliable, especially if you're not really familiar with the parent. Many is the shocked mom or dad after believing, "Freeman's mom said she'd be home the whole time," or, "The father sounded pretty strict," or, "They seemed like really nice people." The best interviews don't verify someone's reliability after five minutes.

*When* will you be home? Of course, this is one you will often answer yourself. The *when* may depend upon the who, what, and where. Further, a broken *when* will render all other Ws irrelevant for a while, as you reconsider the range of Liberty's social freedom.

*Why* are you going? The toughest W to verify. "Because I like being with my friends," or some variant, might be acceptable given Walker's answers to the other Ws. Then again, the activity may be okay but the motive is suspect. "I want to go swimming with Brooke"—a good *what* and a passable *who*. "Her boyfriend, Harley, and his biker friends are meeting us there"—a very bad *why*.

All five Ws work in harmony. One unacceptable W can negate four acceptable ones. Also, all Ws must be affirmed with the utmost care. Social freedom is founded upon trustworthiness. It does not automatically accompany age.

Former president Ronald Reagan's advice for monitoring foreign countries applies well to monitoring teens: Trust but verify.

# Old Young

Dear Dr. Ray,

My twelve-year-old thinks she's sixteen. She wants a lot more free-dom than I think is good for her age. How can I convince her she's not sixteen?

*Aging Fast*

You can't—not with only words anyway. Once kids start inching toward double-digit ages, they increasingly think they should be treated older than their age—in freedoms and rights, that is, not in duties and responsibilities. What twelve-year-old says, "Gee, Mom, I think I'm old enough to pay for my own clothes and do my own laundry"?

It's understandable that your daughter wants more than you're willing to give her. Almost all kids want more than their parents know is good for them. And growing up is a push-and-pull over how much we're going to permit when.

> Growing up is a push-and-pull over
> how much we're going to permit when.

Much of your daughter's reaching for sixteen is pushed by society. The popular culture strips children young of childhood. The world around them relentlessly tempts and tells them to be discontent with who they are and what they have. It offers them latitude at ages when their counterparts of a generation or two ago were still content to be at home. All this forces you into hyper-vigilance, striving to give your daughter a few more years of age-appropriate childhood.

So how do you keep a twelve-year-old a twelve-year-old—or a sixteen-year-old a sixteen-year-old, for that matter? By treating her like a twelve-year-old or a sixteen-year-old. By giving and allowing her only what you judge is good for her at her age, no matter what age she is in her mind.

"How can I convince her she's not sixteen?" has two answers. You can't, and you can. You can't in that she seldom will agree with your age-bound decisions. She's a twelve-year-old, and they are noted for not seeing the world a parent's way. You can in that you will make your daughter live as a twelve-year-old, with its freedoms, privileges, and responsibilities.

Most stubborn reality resisters (a.k.a., children) eventually see the wisdom of their older folks. Some take months, some take years, and many become parents.

This is just an example of life being wired backward. Children spend years wanting to be more grown-up than they are, only to one day be grown-up and nostalgically long for the carefree years of youth.

# A Matter of Trust

Dear Dr. Ray,

Two times in two weeks, my fourteen-year-old son was not where he told us he'd be. My husband says two weeks' grounding. I say indefinitely.

*Fooled Me Twice*

I've been married forty years. I have five daughters. I've learned to give the female perspective great weight.

That said, a few questions. Where was your son when he was not where he said? It's one thing to stop at Burger Binge after the game without asking. It's quite another to head to Bambi's party, especially when Mr. and Mrs. Buck aren't home.

Is it safe to assume that your son didn't stop off at church to pray an extra half hour? He headed somewhere he wouldn't have a prayer of being allowed at even if he'd asked on bended knee.

Next question: How do you know you were fooled only twice? You may have been fooled more but were so fooled you never realized you were fooled. Teens usually do more things wrong than they're caught at. Pretty much, doesn't everybody? This isn't being cynical or untrusting of kids. This is accepting reality.

Since a primordial drive of teenhood is for more social movement than parents know is good, opportunity and temptation can mix to overcome a youngster's conscience and fear of penalty.

Where and how often your son has pushed his social boundaries is hard to know, but you did catch him twice in two weeks.

You're vigilant or lucky or both, or he's sloppy or guilt ridden or both. Either way, in the future, you're wise not to presume anything. Find a way to check.

About the grounding: Most parents would side with your husband. If a youngster abuses a privilege, he loses the privilege for some period.

I lean your way. And it's not only because you're a female. Your son broke your trust—deliberately, it sounds. You gave freedom commensurate with your judgment of his character. If he has revealed that you underestimated his judgment, then you are right to rethink your judgment.

One option is open-ended grounding as your son reproves that he can be trusted. Monitor more closely the who, what, when, and where of his social world. Consider a two-week full grounding, followed by a partial grounding for as long as you judge good to emphasize the lesson and to send your son a clear signal.

Raising teens is a lot like controlling a feisty colt. You have to hold the rope tightly and close to his bridle. The more rope between your hand and his head, the less you can direct him anywhere. With both horses and teens, hold the reins close, letting them out by the inch as they settle.

> With both horses and teens,
> hold the reins close, letting them
> out by the inch as they settle.

Some might be uneasy with my comparing adolescent boys and horses. I plead guilty. For one thing, training horses to go where you'd like is easier.

# Trust Yourself First

Dear Dr. Ray,

We supervise our daughter far more than do her friends' parents. She's a good kid, but we still keep a close eye. How do we answer, "You just don't trust me"?

*The Hawks*

A short answer: "I trust you. I don't trust the world." A longer answer, though, I suspect, your daughter probably won't accept any better than my pithy sound bite.

"Oh, but I do trust you. I trust that you are fifteen. And I trust that fifteen-year-olds think like fifteen-year-olds. And I trust that there will be situations that, for all your experience, you'll be unsure how to handle. And I trust that with time, I'll allow you to experience more. And I trust that you'll believe me when I tell you I'm doing this out of love and to protect you, a most precious gift from God."

Tell me, how could your daughter not be moved by so much trust?

If Faith continues to call your vigilance distrust, so be it. It's not that you don't recognize her maturity. It's that you recognize its limits. Faith is trying to make you feel guilty by turning a positive—protection—into a negative—disrespect.

Why are kids so quick to take our loving supervision personally? For one, both young and old are quick to take another's behavior personally. For another, teens more so are quick to misunderstand parents. Therefore, your daughter sees your boundaries as not giving her enough credit. You just don't realize yet how downright grown-up she is. Thus, the problem, dear parent, lies in your misperception, not in her youth.

"You just don't trust me" may be true. You don't always trust her. Incomplete trust isn't a bad thing, socially or psychologically. It's recognizing reality. The most trusting parent sees the limits of a child's judgment, experience, and character. The most mature fifteen-year-old is still a fifteen-year-old.

> Incomplete trust isn't a bad thing,
> socially or psychologically.
> It's recognizing reality.

By "trusting" their kids prematurely, other parents can feed Faith's exasperation. That is, if all of those grown-ups are more trusting than you, you are the suspicious one. Are they all wrong? If this were a game, the score would be 23—other parents—to 2—you and your spouse.

Were the score even 123 parents to 2, it would be irrelevant. Good parenting is not by consensus. If you believe Faith's friends have too much freedom, then you'll give less—sometimes much so, knowing that Faith won't always understand why. Someday she will, and that's what really matters.

The only foolproof way to convince your daughter that you trust her completely is to allow her all the freedom she wishes. Is it worth going that far to be understood?

# Under Contract

Dear Dr. Ray,

What do you think about behavior contracts with kids?

*Outbargained*

That depends. Who will do your negotiating? Does your attorney specialize in family law? Is there a thirty-day notice of termination? An out clause?

Family therapists like behavior contracts: written agreements between parents and children laying out each party's responsibilities and the terms for breaching the agreement.

Contracts come with both assets and liabilities. Perhaps their main drawback is when they are used for compromise between "equals" — parent and child.

Dawn is appealing for an open curfew. Parents counter with midnight. Contract says: Meet somewhere near the middle, say 2:00 a.m.?

In the legal world of contracts, each party negotiates his best position. In the family world of contracts, parents should set most of the terms, as they are — and should be — the governing authority.

---

In the family world of contracts, parents should set most of the terms, as they are — and should be — the governing authority.

---

If you judge midnight to be reasonable, then bargaining points might be: (1) What privileges can Dawn receive for honoring midnight? (2) What are the consequences for ignoring midnight? (3) What are exceptions to the midnight clock?

Kids are skilled negotiators. Their bartering chops are honed from years of redefining words and proposing options.

A smart contract has time limits. Don't lock yourself into terms that, despite youthful impulse, can't be rendered null and void. What if Dawn finds loopholes in the agreement? Can it then be rescinded?

Contracts are not without their benefits also.

First, they codify terms. Less fuzziness leads to less haggling over details. Is midnight still in force on the Saturday that switches to Daylight Savings Time? What if Dawn is home by 11:59 but sits in the driveway until 12:37?

Second, contracts legislate consistency. What if Perry cooperates and what if he doesn't is in writing. It's preset. It doesn't have to be settled after every situation.

Third, contracts help spouses present a more united front. They mutually set down the expectations and their enforcement, thus lessening potential disagreements.

Overall, contracts aren't needed when parents are clear and predictable. The juvenile party knows that the adult party mean what they say, whether in writing or not. Meaning, an oral contract is as binding as a written one.

# Friends of a Feather

Dear Dr. Ray,

My sixteen-year-old is becoming friendly with a boy who has a history of social troubles. I'm very uneasy with the association, but he says I can't pick his friends.

*Picky*

You're not picking his friends; you're picking the pool of friends from which he can pick. "You can't pick my friends" is an argument that kids fling so freely—and is echoed by so many "experts"—that it rattles parents. It can make them question their duty to protect a child from his questionable choices.

In fact, you do a lot of picking. You may not micromanage every aspect of your son's life, but you monitor almost all of it: what foods he can eat, what clothes he can wear, what money he has, what hours he can stay awake, what media he can imbibe, and on and on. Indeed, it's your duty to control what tries to enter his world.

> It's your duty to control what tries
> to enter your child's world.

Common sense and experience reinforce that one's peers have power, more so than clothes, money, media, and most all else that parents monitor. During the teen years, poor influences can have outsized influence. Therefore, your instincts to protect are good. Don't second-guess them because of your son's peer-stunting accusations.

Kids need to be social. True. Peer relations are a key part of maturing. True. Children can instinctively sort through who is good to be with and who is not. False.

That humans are social beings in no way means that socializing, in and of itself, is always good for humans. It matters greatly with whom one is socializing.

A parallel can be drawn to literacy. Some argue that reading is so good for a child that what he reads is secondary, as long as he is reading something. No, bad reading can shape one badly. Bad friends can do the same.

If you judge this friend to be a poor associate for your son, then, no matter what your son or some experts counter, set your boundaries. They may be absolute—no association with Freeman whatsoever—though tough to monitor at school. Or Freeman may be welcome at your home, where he will be within eye- and earshot. Or you, your son, and Freeman can be a threesome to events. This will excite both boys, I'm sure.

You'll probably not have to worry about the contact very long, however. If Freeman has unlimited social liberty, he's not about to curtail it by coming into your world or your son's.

# Date and Age

Dear Dr. Ray,

My oldest daughter is fifteen. Most of her friends have boyfriends. What do you think is a good age at which to allow children to start this?

*Aging Fast*

When they're married. And only with their spouses.

Opposite-sex involvement—made much earlier and easier by the ubiquitous smartphone—is much harder for parents to oversee these days. Some guidelines:

1. Most kids are involved way too early.
2. Don't use the cultural "average age" to make your decision.
3. Start slow and supervised.
4. When in doubt, hold off.
5. Nothing is to be gained by premature opposite-sex relationships through the phone, games, dances, or group gatherings.

Life Truth Number 204: If you act unlike most, you will be misunderstood by most. Suppose you've decided opposite-sex discussions will begin when your daughter turns fifteen. Now, back in the old days—the early 2000s—you'd meet resistance mainly from your daughter. What is different these days is that you are almost as likely to be questioned by your peers.

If you act unlike most, you will be
misunderstood by most.

"These are different times. This is not when you and I were
growing up. These kids grow up so much faster nowadays. You
can't protect them forever. You can't wrap a moral bubble around
them; they have to deal with life."

"If you make kids too different, they'll feel like weirdoes who
don't fit in. Then they'll get resentful and rebellious. I had a friend
in California whose neighbor's boss had a son whose cousin's
best friend wasn't allowed to date until he was seventeen, and I'll
tell you, he turned his back on everything his parents had tried
to teach him. When he got to college, he ran like a wild animal."

People do have a penchant for arguing by exception. But a
recent survey suggested that if a child has a first "date" between
the ages of eleven and thirteen, he or she has an 80 percent prob-
ability of being sexually active during senior year in high school.
First date at age fourteen leads to a 50 percent chance. First date
at age sixteen, 20 percent chance. What chance would you take?
What chance is much of society taking?

Key factors to consider in granting any type of dating freedom
are the child's moral maturity, independence of thought, history of
conduct in other social settings, strength of will, social judgment,
choice of friends, responsibility toward schoolwork and respect
for authority. I figured if I make the list long enough, my kids
wouldn't be eligible to date until they move out.

As an aside, "dating" is so last week. Does anyone still ask another "out," pick the person up, drive there together, and converse
face-to-face for like more than an hour? Ewww!

Once confident that your daughter has met your standards, sit her down and tell her how much you admire who she is and then, "Just three more years and you can date."

Just kidding. Sort of.

# One Call from Your Cell

Dear Dr. Ray,

All of my fourteen-year-old daughter's friends have smartphones. She's pushing hard; I'm holding out; Dad is yielding.

*Just My Hang-Up?*

The average age of first-time smartphone possession is now ten, and the trend is heading younger. At age fourteen, your daughter is in a miniscule minority. So far, there are no reports of babies having smartphones—yet. But to borrow from Bishop Fulton Sheen: Right is right even if no one is right. Wrong is wrong even if everyone is wrong.

Parents ask me, "What is the single biggest obstacle to my raising a child with faith and morals?" Hands down, give the child a smartphone, early and unfettered.

The social and moral risks are heavy and relentless. Social media can take over a child's world, misshaping self-concept and emotions. Research is clear: The more time spent in the Internet social unreality, the more anxiety and depression, especially among girls. Among boys, one survey found that between the ages of eleven and nineteen, either deliberately or accidentally, more than 90 percent of boys have viewed pornography.

Space here limits the whole scope of soul-misshaping effects of smartphone obsession. My book *Raising Upright Kids in an Upside-Down World* goes into far more detail. Fortunately, voices are gathering urging control, monitoring, and delay.

Parents are shell-shocked at their child's intense, near unraveling, emotional reaction to losing the phone even for a short time, due to misusing it. It sends them a clear signal of how much of their teen's existence is wrapped around something a little larger than a deck of cards.

A recent television series listed the smartphone as the invention most life-altering. In just over a decade, it has become nearly everyone's fixed companion. My eighty-year-old mother, only a few years prior an inveterate phone resister, couldn't imagine leaving the house without her ever-ready link to everybody.

The trouble lies not in the technology itself but in whose hands it's held. It can take anyone of any age anywhere anytime. And it can bring the whole world — its very good and its very evil — to anyone.

> Smartphones bring the whole world — its
> very good and its very evil — to anyone.

Cell phones enable kids to reach out and touch someone — lots of someones — known and unknown. How's a parent to know whom Belle is talking to about what, when, where, and how much? Surveys say the average user sends and receives many thousands of texts per month. Cell phones open up to kids a whole new peer world that parents have a cell of a time monitoring.

Most kids won't use a cell phone to break the law, buy drugs, or cheat on school tests. It's the everyday intrusion that removes them from those personally present. Everyone is singing "Happy Birthday" to Grandma, and Tally is off texting seventy words a minute.

Teens have all sorts of immature ideas about what is cool, what is romantic, what is desirable, what is permitted, what can be risked.

Teens also can be pretty sheeplike. They are prone to follow the flock. Cell phones are the perfect medium for teens to exchange endless peer talk—some good, some bad, all private.

"I want to know where my son is." How do you know for sure? Can you trace the location of the call? A call can come from anywhere. And even if the phone can be tracked, it can be left anywhere while its owner is elsewhere.

"It's so convenient. Alexander and Belle can call me when necessary." Okay, purchase a phone with a ten-minute monthly limit. Or one that can only receive or call preprogrammed numbers. Or give the phone to Alexander only for particular activities or reasons.

"It's for safety." Refer to the above options.

When you do decide to award a phone, some conditions will reduce the chances of misuse or "addiction":

1. No phone in the bedroom or after 9:00 p.m. Kids nightly take their phones to bed. Late hours? Sleep deprivation? School sleepiness?

2. No phone during meals, visits to relatives, church, or anywhere else you don't want its presence.

3. Install safeguards. Space again limits all the options, as there are so many. "Safe" phones are available—no Internet and only selected apps. Phone timers allow only certain hours of use. "Pairing" your phone to a child's allows you to see on yours everything that comes and goes on hers. Surveys have found that only a minority of parents use safeguards, trusting their children to use the phone morally and responsibly until . . .

4. To find the safeguards most convenient and effective for you, do an Internet search on your phone.

I am not a back-to-nature psychologist, recommending no cell technology whatsoever. But I strongly advise that you resist the cultural-flow cell-phone age and freedom. The fact that 90 percent of kids above fourteen have a cell does not make it smart. Someday your daughter will have her own phone, and that day should not be when 92 percent of her age group has one but when you judge her mature enough to use it wisely. When she's married?

One last call: Ask your daughter, "Why do you want a phone so much?"

Savvy kids cite the safety and keep-in-touch reasons that parents cite. They know what they're supposed to say. Give your daughter the above answers. Then wait to see what her real arguments are.

You might hear some reasons that will convince you further to hold the line. Get your husband to listen in. Call him on his phone if you have to.

# Driving Ambition

Dear Dr. Ray,

The big D—driving—is coming up fast. My son has been riding me about it since he turned fifteen.

*Nervous Wreck*

Driving: to teens, on entitlement; to parents, a privilege. To teens, new freedoms; to parents, new worries. To teens, passage to adulthood; to parents, a passage to lost sleep.

Teens live by the numbers. Indy thinks that since he has reached x years, certain rights must follow. "I'm sixteen [or whatever the state's legal age is], so I should be able to drive." To paraphrase Descartes, "I am, therefore I drive."

As I told my teens, "Sixteen is the minimum age at which the state tells me I can think about this. It is not the age it must happen." Sixteen is only a number, like four or eleven or thirteen and a half.

Nonetheless, because the state rules it legal, or because most other parents agree with the state, or because teens are so harddriving about it, most parents yield, even if their better judgment says, "Stop." Many would prefer to let Betsy mature more before getting wheels, but they relent under the pressure.

At one time, I had five children approaching or fresh into driving age—nineteen, seventeen, sixteen, sixteen, fifteen and a half—and as one who's also learned lots from years of riding shotgun with other parents, let me offer some guardrails:

*What matters is not the legal age.* What matters is the social and moral age. What is the level of trustworthiness? How cooperative is he at home? At school? With chores? How does he treat you? His siblings? Has he been responsible in matters less than driving? The best predictor of how Carla will guide a car is how she's guided her life up to the present.

---

What matters is not the legal age.
What matters is the social and moral age.

---

Parents often permit a license after years of behavior that has been difficult, disrespectful, and demanding. The concession is "Well, she is old enough, so I guess it's time." Or, "It will be unlivable around here unless I let her."

*Don't ignore your better judgment because of pressure*—from others, your child, or your schedule. A privilege as far-reaching as driving asks for much prudence and patience before being permitted. If in doubt, think longer, then delay.

*Be ready to reassess your decision.* After weighing everything, you believe Van is now old enough to drive. (He is twenty-four.) What if he mishandles the privilege?

Most parents ground the child or take the keys. For serious misuse, a week or two without wheels may not be sufficient. Time-limited grounding may have to yield to open-ended supervision. Only when you are confident in Van's change of direction does the door of the car open again.

On license day, along with congratulations, inform Edsel that this is not his permanent license, as the state calls it. It is still a temporary permit, based upon his responsibility and maturity.

- *Implement a "good student" clause.* Only sustained good grades lead to sustained license. Grades drop, license drops.
- *A clean car is a drivable car.* That means Walker keeps it that way, not you.
- *Gas and insurance cost money.* Household cooperation is necessary to help pay operating costs.
- *Respect is a two-way street.* Permission to drive is a parent's respect for the child's unfolding independence. A child's respect toward the parent is a parallel response.

Teens and most adults view driving as more age related than character related. Age is the lesser factor. It comes down not to what year Axel was born but what year he has grown up.

# Teens Are Like Airplanes

Dear Dr. Ray,

My teenagers are fourteen and sixteen. We disagree over curfew. Suggestions for establishing reasonable times? And how best to enforce them?

*The Timekeeper*

A safe assumption: Your idea of a reasonable curfew is earlier than your teens', not the other way around. I did read about a fifteen-year-old who argued for an earlier curfew than his parents set. Last I heard, he was being studied at a leading university's Center for Unearthly Phenomena.

Parents and teens do sometimes agree on what is a fair time to be home. They just talk different time zones. Parents can live with midnight, the kids too, but we're talking midnight Eastern Standard Time and they're talking midnight Pacific Time.

> Parents and teens do sometimes agree
> on what is a fair time to be home.
> They just talk different time zones.

Adolescents believe, unlike their parents—who have lived just a shade longer but who, in the kids' eyes, are no wiser for it—that they can responsibly handle a later curfew, repeating the mantra

"Anything we can do at 1:00 in the morning we can do at 1:00 in the afternoon." True. But we oldsters know that the potential for trouble and craziness rises steadily with each minute into the wee morning hours. As previously said, it isn't so much that we don't trust our kids; it's more that we don't trust the others who are out and about at that hour.

Will kids understand and willingly accept your reasoning? If they do, kiss them. It's not respectable teenhood to agree happily to come home before one is ready. Teens like being out of the folks' eye- and earshot, especially at night. Something about the dark appeals to their independent streak.

You could seek the kids' input about what they think is fair—a four-letter word they like to fling around. If curfew is mutually settled, compliance is probably better, as Faith had some say in it. If, however, after sixty-two hours of nonstop negotiating through a federal mediator, you and she are still three hours apart, what is fair is your ruling.

Some parents set consistent curfews—for example, 9:00 p.m. on weekdays, midnight on weekends. Exceptions periodically are based on flexible factors as special occasions, amount of supervision, or Gardiner's promise to mow the lawn for the next three years without being asked. So if Barbie is double-dating with her boyfriend's parents to the ballet (right!); curfew then might be extended to 1:30 a.m.

On the other hand, if Oliver wants to use your two-day-old van to take his girlfriend to a quadruple feature at a drive-in somewhere across the state line, you might move curfew to 8:00 p.m, an hour before the first movie starts.

Some parents have no set curfews, instead judging each activity on its merits or lack of. This does carry the potential for more arguments, as each request can become a rowdy back-and-forth.

It's tempting to allow an unwise curfew because "there's not even enough time to get anything to eat after the game," or "not a single guy in the whole school will ask me out because I have to be in so early," or "come on, Dad, these are different times than when you were growing up." Indeed they are. All the more reason for smart curfews.

Kids will present all manner of rationales to gain more hours. Most of the time, this is not a sign that you are unloved, disrespected, or thought unfair. You are just plain disagreed with.

Even though sticking to a curfew can cause agitation, it'll help you sleep better. An adolescent's night arrival, followed by the sound of a key in the door, almost always prompts a lying-in-bed-wide-awake parent to begin nodding off.

Now, the enforcement question: How can you ensure that Hope will abide by her curfew? Answer: You can't. The best discipline won't guarantee that she will obey. Only she can guarantee that. You can do much, however, to make it more likely she will.

It would be uncool, at least inconvenient, for you to shadow Hope everywhere to escort her home on time. You would stand out conspicuously at any teen gathering. Your jeans aren't faded enough or properly torn. And please, don't dance.

Some enforcement options:

1. Bad grammar aside, a privilege abused is a privilege losed. A time-ratio rule: for each fifteen minutes late, one day of grounding. You choose the days. Let Dawn choose, and she'll pick Monday afternoon and Wednesday evenings.

2. Old-fashioned grounding still works—although it's always confused me how often we feel we can't live in the same house with that kid for one more minute, and then we turn around and force her to stay home.

3. A tighter ratio: Every minute late without a solid, verifiable reason, five minutes come off the time allowed for the next activity. For example, Knight drifts in at 12:36 a.m. with the claim that the electricity in the gym went out for thirty-six minutes (excuse rating: fairly original, too verifiable, overall nice try). Using a one-to-five ratio, 36 x 5 = 180 minutes = three hours earlier Knight has to be in the next time he wants to go somewhere. So, if normal curfew is midnight, next time out, it's 9:00 p.m. Knight responds, "It's not even worth going out then." Probably not.

   Any ratio works: five minutes late costs fifteen; fifteen costs an hour; ten costs ten.

4. Curfew cooperation can lead to curfew relaxation. If Eve goes out and comes in on time, without grousing, multiple times in a row, she can earn some bonus add-on time. The message, as always, is: "Responsibility begets freedom."

In the end, no matter how curfew compliant your teen is, every so often, she'll make you discipline because teens are like airplanes. Their scheduled arrival time doesn't always coincide with their actual arrival time.

# The Online Bottom Line

Dear Dr. Ray,

If I let them, my kids would live on the computer. I don't think it's a good place to live.

*Virtually Ignored*

Every computer needs a monitor—a really, really good one. What kind of monitor? A parent—a really, really good one. Otherwise, the computer is more than useless; it is treacherous.

> Every computer needs a really
> good monitor—a parent.

Most parents permit kids to head into computer world with no boundaries other than the child's self-monitoring. A survey found that only 17 percent of parents oversee their kids' computer use.

Like the smartphone—a computer in the hand—it allows a child to visit anyone anyplace and see anything—good or bad, helpful or hurtful, friend or fiend. Something limitless needs impenetrable safeguards. Anything less is like putting a machine gun in the hands of a three-year-old. The potential for danger and pain is ever lurking.

I'm no computer geek. For two years I wore my garage-door opener so people would think I had a pager. But I am a child-rearing geek. So here are a few basic commands to make you a better monitor:

1. *A tight filter is a must.* If need be, get help installing it—your six-year-old nephew. No safeguard is foolproof. The goal is to screen out as much sleazy, awful stuff as possible. Many parents don't, and they come to feel the regrets.

2. *Use a password to log on, one known only to you.* The computer is opened only by your fingers.

3. *A computer can be linked to a timer,* alowing access only during certain days, hours, or minutes. Let the computer help supervise itself.

4. *Keep the computer(s) visible in a well-traveled, observable place*: the kitchen, dining room, family room. Two of the worst places are the basement and a child's room. A TV in a kid's bedroom is foolish; so, too, is a computer.

5. *Dramatically limit, if not prohibit, communication in chat rooms, personal blogs, and instant messaging.* You can't know with whom they're interacting—and neither can they. And even if you and they do know, it's still a challenge to monitor what is said about what and whom and how it is said.

Just because a technology has exploded onto the scene, that doesn't mean one has to absorb it all, particularly when the one absorbing it has immature judgment. So many parents realize the computer's downsides only after their child has experienced them personally.

Schools assign much work now on the computer. Refer again to commands 1 through 5. Then be more vigilant. Oxford knows you're less likely to watch what he's doing since it's school related.

Check regularly. Not that teens are sneaky or slick—well, okay, some—but the pull to go elsewhere beyond schoolwork is relentless.

Are all of these cautions roundabout ways of crying, "Trash the computer"? No. For better or worse, more of existence is becoming computer-linked every day. But given the computer's unlimited reach, it must have gatekeepers. Otherwise, it won't be our servant; it will be our master.

# 7

# Standing Strong

Good parents have higher standards than their teens do. This is not a revelation: It has been so. It's up to parents to teach children a better way.

Only in the last few generations have good parents met resistance from an unexpected direction: other parents. Those assumed more mature are instead lowering their standards closer to their teens' level. Consequently, the best of parents now must stand stronger, not just with juveniles but with adults.

A theme throughout this book: Great parenting is not consensus parenting. Hold fast to higher standards and closer supervision, no matter how loosely others are holding to theirs. Your children, will prove you right.

# Do Mistakes Make Maladjustment?

Dear Dr. Ray,

I think I read too much. I always wonder if I'm going to do something wrong as a parent, something that will cause emotional problems now or later.

*Tentative*

You are experiencing a haunting fear among parents today: the fear of somehow making a child-rearing blunder that will lay the roots of future psychological damage. More tormenting is that you can't know when or where the damage is going to manifest itself, as it's buried out of sight within a youngster's psyche, festering for years. And when it does show itself, you're left to search for where and how you went wrong.

Seventeen years hence, will Pandora be in some encounter group, along with seven other parolees — she's their leader — talking about you and the low point in her upbringing?

"I've never shared this with anyone. I was five years old. My mother was screaming my full name, first, middle, and last, from the garage, along with words I couldn't understand. When I got to the garage, she ordered, 'Go to your room and don't come out until you're married.' Then she threw my Care Bear into the trash can and covered it with coffee grounds, laughing hideously and promising that she'd never again buy me anything if I couldn't keep it where people wouldn't trip over it.

"I was never quite myself after that. At six, I started counterfeiting school lunch tokens. A year later I wrote my first bad check."

How can you parent, much less relax and enjoy it, under the black cloud that if you miscalculate, misjudge, lose your cool, or slip into any other human miscue, you run the risk of setting in motion a cascade of emotional struggles that will culminate in a social misfit?

Charity won't willingly share with her brother. If you make her, will she grow up resenting him and maybe all males? To get Newton to finish his math homework, you must require that he do so after school before anything else. He fights this rule. Will he be so averse to numbers that he'll be the school's first fifteen-year-old sixth-grade dropout?

Everyday parenthood entails decisions and judgments—so many that you could keep yourself in turmoil second-guessing yourself.

The experts have done much to make parents anxious. A "family specialist" on national television told parents that one of the worst things they could do—leading to all manner of adult turmoil—was to be inconsistent with their children.

What is an innate characteristic of being human? Inconsistency. No one is totally consistent in parenting or in anything else. We may move toward it, but we'll never reach it. And now we're hearing that because we are who we are, our kids will suffer. One mom bemoaned, "Reading all this stuff makes me feel as if the worst thing for a child is a parent."

Reading all this stuff makes me feel as if
the worst thing for a child is a parent.

As children mature, so do parents. We learn from good and bad actions alike. You'll say things you shouldn't. You'll overreact, denying John bathroom privileges for three months because he left his underwear on the towel rack again. Of course, he'll use the paternal defense: "Dad does it!" Then, coming from the garage, you'll both hear, "When you start paying the bills around here, young man, you can leave your underwear anywhere you want!"

In total, you may make more "mistakes" than did your parents, even if you're a better parent. For one, childhoods are getting shorter. Nine-year-olds now face what twelve-year-olds a generation ago—what fifteen-year-olds two generations ago—used to face. The world is fast becoming a tricky, seductive place. If it's harder for a child to grow up, it will be harder for a parent to grow up with him, and more tricky judgments will be made along the way.

For another, as childhoods are getting shorter, parenthoods are getting longer. Not so long ago, after eighteen years or so, the kids vacated the homestead. Nowadays, twenty-six or twenty-seven years after birth, they're still hanging around. They might leave for a couple of years, just to tease you. Soon they're back, though, with their friends and their laundry, at three in the morning. "Guys, we can stay here a little while, a couple of years anyway. Mom will feed us between washing the white and color loads. She likes to do that kind of stuff."

Parenthood is not for the faint of heart. It's as demanding as it is rewarding. In the end, the whole picture is what counts. And for most of us, the good moves far outnumber the bad.

# Pick Your Battles?

Dear Dr. Ray,

I've heard "Pick your battles" with children, but I'm not sure exactly what that means or how to do it.

*Battle-Fatigued*

"Pick your battles" is a buzzphrase among expert types. It holds malleable meanings. Whether it's helpful depends on how and where you practice it.

At one level, "pick your battles" makes parenting sense. Much of what any child does, even if irksome, is not wrong. It is not immoral, hurtful, defiant, dangerous, or irresponsible. It is kid junk, the stuff of childishness.

A personal scenario: While all traveling in our van, several of our children, usually the younger and more tone-deaf, would decide to sing. Some might call this the melody of youth, but each sang a different tune, different songs, with made-up words, with poor timing, and with gusto. While grating to our ears, they weren't doing anything wrong, at least for the first thirty-six seconds or so. They were just being kids, however goofy. But if my wife or I were to ask them to tone it down to a dull roar or to stop so we could converse without yelling, they'd better, not only for our sanity but to show respect. We, the parents, had a right to settle the chaos, little battle or not.

Another meaning of "pick your battles" drastically undercuts parents. It says: Stand firm on the major moral stuff, but be flexible on the minor moral stuff, particularly if your youngster is overall a "pretty good kid."

Your thirteen-year-old son, Sting, wants to catch a rock concert with his buddy Ringo. By today's standards, the concert is relatively benign. The group, "Kids in Charge," has only two minor felonies and a pending drug probe. You're against it. Sting's too young; there is no adult supervision; the scene is just too crazy.

Now, some experts (probably those without thirteen-year-olds) would advise: Find mutual meeting ground. Don't insist it all be your way because Sting could resent your lack of trust. He can go if he takes a phone and checks in. Or maybe Ringo's dad will go too. If the rock concert is a no-go under any conditions, how about a paid trip to three movies of Sting's choice instead? After all, you don't want to be rigid about all this.

Actually, you do want to be rigid. This, to you, is an important battle. When your child's well-being is at stake, if someone tells you to pick your battles, ignore him.

> When your child's well-being is at stake, if someone tells you to pick your battles, ignore him.

An everyday battle: Rocky torments his sister Adrian. Since sibling squabbling is called "normal," shouldn't you overlook some of it? Minor assaults—words or putdowns—are skirmishes that can be ignored, as long as there is no slapping.

Is it wrong or isn't it to mistreat someone? If you think it is, then sibling respect is a battle to pick and to win, no matter how "small" the wrong.

One last salvo: When you pick your battle, don't battle. Enforce your decisions with calm discipline, not debating or over-reasoning. The sooner the "battle" is over, the fewer battles you will face, as Patton learns what battles you will pick.

# Rebelling without a Cause

Dear Dr. Ray,

What do you think about the notion that if parents are "too strict" or put their moral standards too high, ultimately a child will rebel?

*Strict but Wavering*

Of all the parent-assaulting, authority-undercutting notions that blanket the child-rearing landscape today, this one gets my vote for ranking among the worst. How's that for sugarcoating my answer?

Certainly if parents are dictatorial and unloving, they risk raising a child who could ignore or challenge their standards with age. The saying is "Rules without relationship can breed rebellion."

There is a critical difference between strong parenting with love and strong parenting without love. The warning is that no matter how much you love, if you expect too much good behavior or are too different from the crowd, you're asking for resentment and resistance. Your lofty standards will be the very thing fomenting unruliness. This nutty notion feeds the stereotype of the "preacher's kid," who, as everyone knows, is the sneakiest, most morally profligate kid in the congregation. Truth is, most preacher's kids are more moral than the norm. False notions are sustained by the exceptions that do fit the stereotype.

Some kids will rebel against high standards regardless of the strength of their parents' love. As long as free will lives, there are no parenting guarantees. But again, more often than not, rebellion is only temporary. Eventually, most teens will return to what they were taught younger.

This pushed-upon-parents philosophy is paralyzing. It can keep you from being resolute in the ideals you know are right. After all, Dorothy already thinks she has the Wicked Witch of the West for a mother and Attila the Hun for a father. So you'll only make things worse by being "too controlling." Compromise your moral position every so often so as not to be too inflexible.

Once upon a time, parents instinctively understood that it was wise to enforce high standards. Now this instinct is being challenged. Set your moral bar too high, the novel wisdom says, and a youngster's resistance is confirmation that you're being too earnest about this whole parenting thing. On the contrary, it's confirmation that you're the parent and your child isn't.

---

> Once upon a time, parents
> instinctively understood that it was
> wise to enforce high standards.

---

But what if you're far above the parenting norm in your supervision, in the limits you set, in the respect you expect? Won't your kids draw comparisons? Of course. They'll resist more so than they would if they saw more people thinking as you do.

Because you set your moral sights high for both you and your children doesn't mean you'll reach them consistently. That's kids. Indeed, that's us. Over time, however, your high standards will become standard for your family. And other parents will wonder how you are raising kids who aren't as rebellious as theirs.

# Face the World, Kid!

Dear Dr. Ray,

I want to keep my kids innocent and to give them longer childhoods. But I hear, "You can't protect them forever. That's a real world out there. They have to learn to deal with life."

*Cautious Mom*

Yes, you can't protect them forever. Yes, that is a real world out there. And yes, they do have to learn to deal with life. How is any of that relevant raising your children at your pace and not the world's?

What you are hearing is another in my top-ten list of nonsense notions undercutting good parents today. Mindlessly repeated by so many so often, it has assumed the illusion of child-rearing truth. It is so just because everybody says it is.

A couple of generations ago, it was thought intrusive and impolite for someone to give you their unasked-for opinions about your child-rearing. Protecting kids—socially, morally, and emotionally—was considered an ultimate good. It was a duty of grown-ups to guard children from ugly and immoral stuff while their morality was developing. Keeping kids innocent was a sign of responsible parenting. Soon enough, a youngster would meet what was out there after childhood.

The last generation or two, however, has regressed toward "enlightenment." It is now said to be more farsighted to guide kids through seamy reality as it assails them. What's more, if you delay too long, when the child finally does confront the "real world," whatever that means, he will be shell-shocked, psychologically speaking. He'll be overwhelmed or seduced by evil or crushed into despair. His very innocence will be his undoing.

Who is better able to navigate temptations and challenges: a mature child or an immature child? Who is more able to cope with life's realities: a moral eight-year-old or a moral eighteen-year-old?

The opposite of innocence is not maturity; it is worldliness. And worldliness doesn't equip a child to cope with the world. It makes him more likely to be comfortable with it.

> The opposite of innocence is not maturity; it is worldliness.

Most of those accused of being overprotective are not stunting their children emotionally, nor are they bulldozing all of life's obstacles and frustrations from their path. Their protectiveness is morally moved. They are shielding their kids from situations and people who could overwhelm their judgment or their young consciences.

Only too late do many parents realize that they weren't protective enough. Over and over again, my experience with families has taught me this truth: Far more children struggle as adults not because they grew up too slowly but because they grew up too fast.

Stand strong, Mom. Protect innocence. Lay a solid moral base before the world questions it. Your "overprotectiveness" will be a gift to your children's futures.

# He's Just a Kid

Dear Dr. Ray,

Is it my imagination, or are more and more parents getting criticized by others for disciplining their kids?

*Getting Criticized*

If it's your imagination, then you and I share the same fantasy.

A mother told me of this experience. She and her two daughters (ages twelve and fourteen) were at a pool party. Come dusk, the hostess asked the parents to shepherd the kids from the pool. Several parents took up bargaining positions poolside and began to ask, plead, and promise red Corvettes in reward for cooperation.

Mom said she caught her daughters' attention and, with her hand, motioned for both to exit the water. At which the girls climbed out, dried off, and sat down. The other parents, observing the contrast between her girls' cooperation and theirs, were floored. Mom told me, "We heard we were the talk of the party after that."

What was the talk? If you surmise something like, "How did she do that?" you would be as wrong as I was. Mom was accosted with "It's not normal for kids that age to be so cooperative. We wonder what goes on at home for them to be so afraid of you."

What was once a valued, respected result of good discipline—a child's cooperation—was being interpreted as a bad thing, as some kind of autocratic intimidation. The girls weren't cooperating with their mother's legitimate authority; no, they were Stepford kids, in robotic lockstep to the she-tyrant's dictates.

How did healthy discipline become so questionable? The answers to that question would take us far beyond the bounds of this book. Here are a few, though.

*The experts.* They consistently preach that words, reason, and negotiation are the means to guide children. If these fail, discipline is a last resort, but savvy parents shouldn't have to do much of that. Because this is "proper" child raising, those who are strong parents are seen as throwbacks, parenting barbarians who don't grasp how autocratic they are.

*The culture.* It is far less respectful of authority than a few generations ago. Authority from anyone—parents, teachers, police, military, employers, the Church—is regarded as stifling personal autonomy and expression. Authority should thus always be questioned, particularly when it enforces good but unwanted rules.

*Child-development theories.* Due to their age, adolescents are expected to be uncooperative and headstrong.

So says up-to-date child-rearing theory. Therefore, any child who becomes more likable as she approaches fourteen, or respects her folks, or enjoys their company, or matures smoothly might be a bit of an aberration, not quite "teen normal."

One counter to this myth is illustrated by homeschooled kids. Because they are less soaked in the peer group's mentality and ways, they don't seem to become quite so pop-defined as "teenagers."

So it's not all in your head. Good discipline isn't as universally admired as it once was. Be confident that you're on the right track, despite others' critiquing you. Your children will show them your way is the right way.

# An Army of One

Dear Dr. Ray,

My kids (boy, thirteen; girl, fifteen) tell me often how much more their friends are allowed to do. And they're right. Their friends are allowed to do more—lots more.

*Feeling Alone*

Back in the Mesozoic era—the mid-1970s—when we threw other parents' ways at our parents, they knew it was mostly bluff. Fact was, many, if not most, parents were somewhat alike in their practices. So when we tried to manipulate Mom by citing Dawn's mom, who lets Dawn set her own bedtime, she was pretty secure in countering, "Well, Dawn's mom isn't your mom; I am." Or, "When you live at Lucky's house, you can do what he does." Or the classic: "If Marlin jumps in the lake, are you going to jump in too?"

Nowadays, as more parents get more lax, stronger parents are feeling more peerless. Further, this "guilt by comparison" tactic is no longer ploy; it's reality. Any youngster, without conducting one tracking poll, can cite ten or twelve families whose ways are more kid-friendly than yours. And since kids judge quality parenting by the numbers, you are supposed to feel pretty out of touch.

To avoid being bullied by the "You're not mainstream" charge, hold fast to these rules:

1. *There are parents out there who think as you do.* They may not be visible to you, as some, too, may be keeping a low profile to avoid being targeted as "too strict" or

"too controlling." Even if your teens are aware of these cave dwellers, they are not about to identify them to you. When have you been regaled with "But, Mom, Gabby has no cell phone, gets only three hours of TV per week, and does chores until noon every Saturday. I think her parents are just too cool"?

2. *Consensus parenting is not wise parenting.* The majority too often doesn't provide a good example. If your way isn't aligned with the group's, it may be that your way is better. It's statistics: The higher up you go, the less you are like others.

3. *Numbers indicate conformity, not correctness.* If 83 percent of thirteen-year-olds receive more than your son's five-dollars-per-week allowance, or if 96 percent of fifteen-year-olds have their own rooms, so? (as my sister would say to me). Your judgments are based upon your life, your morals, your family, and your kids. You're not wrong because most choose differently from you. You may be quite right being one in a hundred, given your goals. Then again, just being the parent most often makes you right.

4. Your kids may try casting you as a lone wolf, but that doesn't mean they're always running with the pack. Somewhere in their minds may lurk, despite all the bluster and recriminations, gratitude for your tough but caring stance. In the meantime, their reaction might be upset, but their delayed reaction may be security and respect. How delayed? Till they have teenagers? Actually, it could be happening even as they accuse, though they'd never admit it.

An axiom of statistics: The really good and the really bad are really uncommon; they're well out of the normal range. Apply that to parenting: The better you strive to be, the less "normal" you are.

---

An axiom of statistics: The really good
and the really bad are really uncommon.

---

One more reassurance: A good home is not a place of strict rules, unyielding limits and arbitrary dictates. Your standards are taught within the embrace of love, warmth, and togetherness. These eventually soften and likely eliminate any lingering teen resentment over your "extreme" way of child-rearing.

Your kids may judge your parenting now by their feelings. But the most accurate judgment is what they think ten years from now.

# Mom's the Boss

Dear Dr. Ray,

My dad was a strong authority during my childhood. In my family, I'm the strong authority. How common is this?

*Mom*

One thing's for sure: It's more common than it used to be. More moms are telling me—usually in exasperation—that they are the disciplinarians in their homes. They set the limits, the structure, and the rules.

"I know my discipline style isn't the greatest. I tend to talk too much, negotiate, and nag, but at least I'm trying—unlike Disney Dad or Mr. Oblivious or Mr. Laissez-Faire or Mr. 'Honey, I was that way when I was a kid, and I turned out okay.'" Some wives then may think, "Can we vote on that?"

During presentations, when I speak about Mom as the disciplinarian, I watch women's elbows meet men's ribs, knowing glances from mate to mate, sheepish husbandly smiles, and "This shrink has you pegged" wifely looks.

Guys, next time you hear your wife locked in a verbal battle with a child, don't sit BarcaLounging in the other room, thinking, "If I close my eyes, I can't tell which one of them is the twelve-year-old." Get up, enter the scene, and pull the plug. "That's not just your mom you're talking to that way. That's my wife. I'm going to ask your mom and my wife what she wants me to do about this. And then I'm going to do more."

Make this a practice, and your wives will feel protected. Sometimes I would hand my boys a couple of bucks, telling them, "Go give your mother grief. I'll be right in." Just teasing. I didn't really have to pay them to give her grief.

However frustrating it may be as lead disciplinarian, that comes with discipline leverage. Suppose you ground Mercedes for some infraction. Dad is passively unsupportive or actively opposed. Either way, you still have leverage. Who does the taxiing? Who cooks meals? Who washes the clothes? Even if Mom works outside the home, in many families she still does much of the domestic care. And that gives her the discipline clout.

If Dad doesn't support the grounding, is he willing to take Mercedes to practice? Will he wash her uniform? Will he pack her lunch? Will he take her to babysit?

I'm not advocating causing marital strife. It's a fact, however, that when Mom sets most of the expectations and rules, automatically she controls most of the consequences. And when you have those, you don't need to overtalk and negotiate. You have the means.

Men, even if you think your wife's style can be too wordy or emotional, that does not diminish her God-given authority. She's still Mom, no matter how frustrated she might become. Besides, if she gets more support from you, she will be less frustrated.

You will then be better able to tell which one is the twelve-year-old.

# Attitude of Gratitude

Dear Dr. Ray,

My fifteen-year-old daughter embarrassed herself and me at her birthday party. She acted very ungrateful for some of her gifts. How can I teach her to be more appreciative of all she has?

*Grateful for an Answer*

Give her less. That's my short answer, but I'll give you more. Happy birthday.

There's a direct relationship between possessions and gratitude: The more kids get, the less they appreciate it. Because of personality differences, the relationship is not perfect, but it's pretty predictable.

Since your daughter's ingratitude showed itself at a birthday party, let's party there for a while. On birthdays, a child is the focal point of divergent streams of gifts. If your daughter's birthday is anything like most these days, the gifts number somewhere between ten and twenty, not counting those given to siblings so they don't feel "left out." I can't fathom how that practice caught on. Siblings *should* feel left out of the gifts; it's not their birthday.

Because your daughter receives so much materially—not only on birthdays—that doesn't mean you have to passively let her have it all. If, in your judgment, it's too much, store some, give some away, and pitch anything objectionable. Your daughter will learn that receiving is a privilege, not a right.

> If, in your judgment, it's too much,
> store some, give some away, and
> pitch anything objectionable.

One mother said, somewhat proudly, "My son has really come a long way in showing gratitude. At his birthday party, he received a toy he already had, and he didn't throw it." That's progress, I guess, but my unspoken question was "And what did you do about those gifts he did throw?" When I later told my wife about this episode, she answered my question: "He would have lost not only his unwanted duplicate but most every other toy he received that birthday." A strong response? Throwing a gift at someone is a strong reaction.

Children don't naturally feel appreciation or gratitude. It comes by slowly learning that possessions are not all entitlements. And when they act so, we must show them it is not so—again, by giving them less than they want and by expecting them to act with gracious appreciation for what they do get. If not, they will lose what they thought was already theirs.

With good conduct, doing often precedes feeling. If grateful behavior is not required, it is unlikely that a grateful attitude will develop.

# Grated by Ingratitude

Dear Dr. Ray,

I'm getting really tired of my fourteen-year-old daughter's complaining attitude. It's particularly frustrating because she doesn't seem to realize how good she has it.

*Grateful for Ideas*

Are you complaining? A law of life, rooted in human nature: We become less grateful the longer we have it good. What starts out as gratitude becomes expectation, becomes demand. Unfortunately, it is tough for anyone, young or old, not to complain more as life gets easier.

> A law of life:
> We become less grateful
> the longer they have it good.

Most parents see their childhood as tougher than their kids'. "When I was a boy, I used to walk eighteen miles to school, uphill both ways, in a foot of nuclear waste. My turn to wear our one pair of shoes came around only every two weeks, and I always gave my turn away. That's the kind of child I was."

"I got up at five o'clock in the morning—two hours after I was allowed to go to bed—and sewed the holes in my one pair of pants.

I split a cornflake for breakfast with my seven brothers, then carried them all to school on my back. And I was grateful for what I had."

What are our kids going to tell their kids? "Five hundred fifty channels. That's all we had when I was a boy. With only a six-foot screen. All of our remote's power buttons were up at the top. You had to stretch your thumb to get to them. That could hurt your wrist."

"One winter, it got so bad that after my mother finished shoveling the driveway, she collapsed halfway up the walk. I had to step over her with my hot chocolate. I almost tripped. I should have sued her."

Truth is, most of our kids do have it better than most of us did—materially and entertainment-wise, that is. So what's a parent to do?

Reassess what your daughter has in perks, social freedoms, and privileges and what she has to do to earn them:

1. *Anything electronic in her room—TV, computer, video games, side-by-side refrigerator/freezer, six-line phone hookup—consider removing,* to a family space or out of the house altogether. Technology is appealing, but it can form Rich's idea of "the good life."

2. *Give less allowance for more chores.* The average kid probably earns about $16 per hour, given the big money he gets for little work. Forge a stronger link between money and help. The help must be willing, not begrudging.

3. *Link social freedoms to maturity and cooperation.* If Freeman wants to attend Lucky's birthday party, before giving him a yes, have him give you a yes to something you'd like done.

4. *Observe Jade's attitude.* If it isn't growing in gratitude, you may want to further reassess what she's getting for

what she's giving. It's easy to think we're not indulgent parents compared with most others.

Our culture is the wealthiest and most materially comfortable in world history. Consequently, raising grateful children takes conscious effort. It doesn't happen as naturally as it would if getting and having more didn't come so easily.

# A Room with a View

Dear Dr. Ray,

Do you think a teenager should have a television in his room?

Spouses Who Disagree

No. In print, my answer looks calm. If you could hear it, it would sound like NOOO!!

A mother told me that her mother bought a TV for her adolescent son. Mom was totally against the idea of a TV in her son's bedroom. Grandma warned, "I gave it to him. It's now his, and if you take it out, you'll deal with me."

To sustain a shaky peace, Mom acquiesced. She asked me if I thought she had the right to deny something someone gives to her son.

I asked, "If a classmate gives your son a bag of marijuana, would you confiscate it?"

"Of course," she said.

"Why?"

"Because it is harmful to him."

"Then you've answered your own question. You have not only the right but the duty to protect your son from bad influences, from wherever they come."

That it came from Grandma complicated the picture, but she boxed Mom into a corner, forcing her to choose between the TV and family peace. Grandma's attitude was "What does this harm?" Too often, that is the guiding question. And if a parent can't find a compelling "harm," she'll find herself yielding to others' pushing, her children's wants, or the cultural flow.

Good parenting is the imparting of morals and character over the better part of twenty years, so the question is not "What does this harm?" The question is "What is its good?"

Is standard TV fare in line with your morals? Will it reinforce what you're teaching? Will it uplift your son's mind and spirit? Does its perspective—toward faith, parents, authority, self-restraint, sex, family—parallel your own? How does it talk to your son, and what does it show him?

How about family time? Will that screen nudge your son closer to the family or further from it? Is TV more entertaining than you are? Will your relationship with your son deepen if you're competing with nearly limitless selections?

Does ready access to private viewing raise your son's time to read, do schoolwork, interact with siblings, do chores, lift weights, converse with you? Will his television broaden his horizons or narrow them?

Our fast-forward culture is making raising children a journey with more twists and turns. Why allow influences into your home that will only work against what you are working for?

If a teenager does not have a television in his room, he is now in the minority, a dwindling one. Too, if parents do not allow a bedroom TV, they are in a dwindling minority. But it's a good minority to be in.

# Disciplining for Others

Dear Dr. Ray,

My son's religion teacher does not have good control of her class. My son, age thirteen, and several other boys act up. She has asked me to discipline him. I think it's her responsibility to maintain order, not mine.

*Not There*

It is, and it isn't. (Don't you just love shrinks?)

If your son's teacher maintained better class order, your son likely would behave better. Since her class order is lacking, you are being asked for discipline backup. You respond that you shouldn't have to and wouldn't have to if she were stronger. Further, you're not on the scene; she is. So she's in a position to correct it. All of this can be legitimately argued until you run headlong into one reality: It is her class, but he is your son.

A friend told me of a scenario similar to yours, except that the teacher made a more stringent demand. Son would not be permitted back unless Mom came and sat in class. My friend asked my opinion.

I answered with a question (another chafing shrink tactic): "Susan, do you want your son to behave only for those people who can control him?"

"Of course not," she said.

"Then you will be the one to teach him to respect all people, including those who aren't strong enough to teach him themselves."

# Standing Strong

A child encounters all manner of discipline styles—some powerful, some pitiful. Grandparents, teachers, babysitters, neighbors, coaches, tutors: All interact with a youngster for better or for worse. Those who have little trouble with Conan make a parent's role that much easier. Those who can't or won't discipline force the parent to step in. There is no way around this.

Behaving for a weak disciplinarian is one sign of a good character (or perhaps a mild or cooperative temperament). Almost all humans—good character or not—will behave for those with the power to control them: police officers, drill sergeants, judges. Most will cooperate with competent disciplinarians: an experienced teacher, a demanding coach, a confident sitter. Only those on their way to exemplary character treat well the pushovers. They have learned from their parents' discipline to respect others, no matter their discipline style.

> Almost all humans will behave for those
> with the power to control them.

It sounds as if you will need to inform your son that you will act immediately and definitely if you get even a whiff that he is disruptive for his religion teacher. Even if every other kid in the class is unruly; you will make sure he is not.

# A Force for Good

Dear Dr. Ray,

Some say that forcing adolescents to attend church against their will only breeds more resistance and eventually could deaden their faith altogether.

*Making Them*

I think it is clichéd, illogical, infinitely stupid, and soul-jeopardizing. (I'm schooled in using soft, affirming language.)

*It is clichéd thinking.* So many shallow notions now dominate the parenting scene, and for little reason other than that they are repeated endlessly and challenged seldom.

For instance, "Don't force a child to do anything he strongly opposes because he could only rebel further." Better to negotiate, compromise or follow his lead, so that what you desire for him will become his desire for him. Push too hard, so goes the warning, and he'll push back harder. He won't accept your way of thinking or doing.

For most of human history, parents instinctively understood that if they wanted a child to embrace their way of life, they had to expose him to it, often against his will. They realized that he was in no position to know better what was for his long-range good. Did all those people in all those times and places get it wrong, and we moderns finally corrected it?

*It is illogical.* Candy shuns healthy food and wants chocolate and cupcakes. By mandating good nutrition, will you shape her into a raging sugar addict who someday will regurgitate all your forced feeding? Suppose a youngster needs long-term medical treatment but resists it, becoming more obstinate with time. If you insist and force him to endure it, will he swallow it for now, persevering only until he is old enough to chuck it all? Or as he matures, will he come to see the need and value of what he had to do?

It is innate to children—adults too—often to resist what is good for us.

*It is infinitely stupid and soul-jeopardizing.* Nothing rivals a child's infinite well-being. Everything else is of no ultimate matter if it does not lead one, step by step, closer to God. To allow a child to retreat from a relationship with the Almighty because he wants to, or because he's bored, or because he sees little value in it, or "because because" is to set a direction the results of which neither he nor you can foresee. It is to allow a child to ignore and potentially reject her very reason for existing.

---

It is innate to children—adults too—
often to resist what is good for us.

---

Further, being present in worship, however reluctantly, allows for a homily to teach, for a prayer to soften—in essence, for God's grace to work. Simply put, the risks of not visiting God far outweigh the risks of temporarily being forced to visit Him.

So it's to church whether a youngster wants to go or not. Then what? We must convey why religion is of infinite worth: the logic, the meaning, the depth of it all. This means we must educate ourselves. We can't give what we don't possess. We must better learn, know, and understand the reasons for worship. As we hand all this to our children, our hope and prayer is that a personal commitment slowly will replace their resistance.

# About the Author

Dr. Ray Guarendi is a Catholic husband, the father of ten adopted children, a clinical psychologist, an author, a professional speaker, and an international radio and television host. His radio show, *The Doctor Is In*, can be heard on the EWTN Global Catholic Radio Network on SIRIUS/XM, iHeart Radio, and more than 500 domestic and international AM and FM radio affiliates. His TV show, *Living Right with Dr. Ray*, can be seen on EWTN and reaches more than 380 million homes in 145 countries and territories.